... And So To School

a study of continuity from pre-school to infant school

Shirley Cleave   Sandra Jowett   Margaret Bate

Report of the project 'Continuity of Children's Experience in the Years 3 to 8'.

NFER-Nelson

Published by The NFER-Nelson Publishing Company Ltd,
Darville House, 2 Oxford Road East,
Windsor, Berks. SL4 1DF.

First Published 1982
© NFER 1982
ISBN 0-85633-245-3
Code 8088 02 1

Printed in Great Britain.

Distributed in the USA by Humanities Press Inc.,
Atlantic Highlands, New Jersey 07716 USA.

Contents

Acknowledgements

This is a report of the project 'Continuity of Children's Experience in the Years 3 to 8', which was sponsored by the Department of Education and Science, and carried out by the National Foundation for Educational Research from 1977 to 1980.

Researchers:	Fay Panckhurst, Marjorie Smith, Shirley Cleave, Janet Holmes, Sandra Jowett
Statistician:	Claire Creaser
Secretary:	Dorothy Merritt

Margaret Bate, who contributed two chapters to this report, was leader of the associated Schools Council project 'Transition and Continuity in Early Education'.

The team wish to thank everyone who made this project possible, especially:

the representatives of local education authorities and social services in the areas where we worked, for their cooperation;

the DES liaison committee for their guidance and advice;

childminders and the staff of nursery schools, day nurseries, playgroups and infant schools where we observed, for their patience and help;

the parents, who answered our questions and allowed us to observe their children;

the target children, who went unconcernedly about their activities and provided us with an insight into their experiences.

CHAPTER 1

Introduction

The project 'Continuity of Children's Experience in the Years 3 to 8', was sponsored by the Department of Education and Science and carried out by the National Foundation for Educational Research in England and Wales between April 1977 and December 1980.

Interest in the continuity of young children's experiences has intensified over recent years as the number and range of facilities for pre-school education and care have increased; nursery schools and classes, playgroups, day nurseries and childminders offer a variety of experiences which have implications for the child coming into infant school.

The proliferation of pre-school settings has largely been the result of social changes and economic constraints. The increasing number of women taking employment outside the home, whether from need or choice, together with the number of parents who desire some pre-school education for their children, have created a demand for more and more places for the under-fives. At the same time, constraints on the expansion of state nursery education provision have encouraged the rapid development of other forms of pre-school care and education in the non-statutory sector.

During the 1950s nursery education faced a long period with no expansion, and the only means of providing for more children was to introduce part-time places instead of full-time attendance. The Ministry of Education *Circular 8/60* told local authorities that there could be no expansion of nursery school provision, but drew attention to the shift system which made more places available at no extra cost. During this post-war period day nurseries provided for a very small proportion of the children needing care. The demand for pre-school places grew, and to help meet this demand, the playgroup movement was started, a number of private nurseries of all kinds came into being, and the number of childminders rapidly increased.

In 1967, as a consequence of the Plowden Report and the Urban Aid programme, local authorities were allowed to expand their provision for young children. A government White Paper, *Education: a Framework for Expansion* (DES 1972), announced a major initiative in the provision of facilities for the under-fives. Ten years of expansion was envisaged, by which time there should be places available for 50 per cent of all three-year-olds and 90 per cent of all four-year-olds. Local authorities were to develop their plans in the light of local conditions. Research programmes were to be set up to monitor the development of the new provision.

During this time there was a re-awakening to the needs of parents and young children. Although further financial constraints prevented a full ten years of expansion and allocation cuts began in 1976/77, various bodies concerned with education research in Britain contributed to the promotion of relevant projects. In the nursery field, studies were made of such aspects as teachers' aims in nursery education (Taylor *et al.*, 1972), current practices in nursery schools and classes (Parry and Archer, 1974), compensatory programmes for socially disadvantaged children (Wood-head, 1976), and communication skills in early education (Tough, 1976).

Work focusing on other forms of provision was also being carried out in the early 1970s. For example, the National Children's Bureau made a study of playgroups in an area of social need (Joseph and Parfitt, 1972), and the Bureau's director was commissioned by the DHSS to provide a source document about the needs of children and how to meet them (Kellmer Pringle, 1974). Several studies were made by the Thomas Coram Research Unit, looking at day care and its effects on pre-school children, and at various aspects of childminding. There was great concern at this time about unsatisfactory childminding which was brought to light by several organizations, and by the work of Brian and Sonia Jackson and others who sought to improve the situation. On the other hand, keenness among dedicated minders was finding expression in the formation of local associations, and in 1977 the National Childminding Association was formed.

A Management Committee to commission and monitor research in connection with the expansion of nursery education was set up by the Department of Education and Science in 1974. In the light of information from their own studies and from the review of current research in the field of early education (Tizard, 1974), this committee determined five areas of priority for further research. These were:

   i) 'What parents want and why' in the realm of pre-school provision
  ii) Coordination of services for the under-fives
 iii) Parental involvement in nursery education
 iv) Continuity and progression in the educational experience of children between the ages of three and eight
  v) The problems associated with the integration of handicapped children into normal classes
(Pre-School Education and Care. June 1975.)

A programme for research in these priority areas was planned. The project 'Continuity of Children's Experience in the Years 3 to 8' was part of this programme and the research was linked with two other projects as a means of broadening the field of study. One project was 'Transition from Home to Pre-School' sponsored by the National Foundation for Educational Research, and the other was an action research project 'Transition and Continuity in Early Education' sponsored by the Schools Council.

It was felt that research in the past had paid little attention to what goes on in the various nursery settings and what the individual experiences of children are, particularly when moving from one provision to another. There was an apparent need for first-hand descriptions of children's early experiences which would increase understanding of what is educationally relevant and significant, and also highlight existing forms of continuity or discontinuity for the children being studied.

Parents, teachers and others concerned with early education had expressed anxiety because the rapid and largely uncoordinated development of pre-school services had sometimes led to incompatibilities between children's experiences in the different stages and types of provision. They were particularly concerned that frequent transitions between provisions with different organizations and learning programmes might cause stress in young children which could be detrimental to their development.

Official joint letters from the DES and DHSS to local authorities also expressed concern and encouraged authorities to set up procedures designed to coordinate the various pre-school services (references No. DES S.214705 of March 1976 and No. S47/24/013 of January 1978).

It was against this background that the project began in April 1977. The years three to eight include those in which a child is most likely to attend some kind of pre-school and those in which he attends infant or first school. During this time he may experience a number of transitions or changes: from home to pre-school; from one pre-school to another from home or pre-school to infant school; from one infant class to the next. Economic and practical constraints necessarily limit the scope of a project and it was not possible to study all the transitions which could occur. Instead it was decided that, since starting school is a necessary transition for almost all young children, continuity could best be studied by looking at what happens when this particular change occurs. Experiences associated with starting school could then be viewed against the wider background of pre-school and infant experiences available to young children.

The project team accordingly set out with two objectives:

1) to provide a detailed description of the experiences of children in all forms of pre-school care and education, and in the infant school;
2) to provide a picture of the individual experiences of a small group of children transferring from a variety of pre-school settings to the infant school.

To achieve these objectives the project was divided into three parts. The first, an exploratory phase, was carried out during the first year and consisted of preliminary visits to all forms of provision, discussions with staff and observations. The purpose of these was to discover the issues which could have a crucial effect on the experiences of young children and to determine the field of inquiry for the research studies which were to follow.

Two research studies were planned: a longitudinal study of the individual experiences of a small sample of children starting school, and a cross-sectional study of the variety of provision available. As time went on it became apparent that it would be more practical to reverse the intended sequence of the research studies and the original plan was modified accordingly. This had the advantage of allowing time for two sub-samples of children to be studied: one sample starting school in September and the other in January. Information gathered from the research studies was expected to reveal similarities and differences between and within types of provision and to illustrate how much children's experiences are likely to be interrupted by moving from one kind of provision to another. The project and its findings are described in detail in the following chapters.

The team worked in liaison with the two other associated projects and researchers from all three met from time to time for discussions. During the early stages, information from the exploratory phase was found useful to the project 'Transition in Early Education'. This was an action research programme which involved working with groups of adults who represented the various types of provision for children from three to eight in several areas of the country. The groups were concerned with identifying and discussing problems which may occur for children on transition and with making recommendations, where appropriate, for ways of harmonizing transition and continuity in the early years.

The other associated project, 'Transition from Home to Pre-School', focused mainly on children starting nursery school or class, and studies were made of children before and after entry.

A joint document linking the findings of all three projects is planned.

Notes

The term 'pre-school' is used throughout this book to denote all types of provision before infant school.

All the people and places referred to are real; only their names are fictitious.

CHAPTER 2

The Exploratory Studies

Preliminary visits, discussions and observations

The first year of the project was spent exploring the field and identifying important issues for research. Discussions took place with infant and nursery advisers in education authorities, and with the coordinators of pre-school provisions in the social services and voluntary sectors. Visits were made to all types of provision for observation and discussions with staff.

The purpose of these visits and discussions was to provide a picture of the sort of experiences a child might have in each of the different settings and of the salient differences between the various types of provision. It was hoped that features which contribute towards continuity or discontinuity would become apparent and that important issues could be identified as focal points for developing a conceptual framework for the two studies which were to follow. Discussions with advisers from the areas selected for study would yield information about the social conditions which influenced the formation of policies for care and education, and about any existing forms of cooperation which might help towards providing continuity of experiences.

Neighbourhood studies were carried out in three areas with differing environments. These were particularly useful in providing a picture of the sort of communication and coordination which existed within each neighbourhood. Two of these studies were quite extensive, both making comparisons between provision in two districts of the same area. This showed the variety of types of provision and the variations within each type.

The first of these comparative studies was on the provision found in two different towns in the same county, one being industrial with a high percentage of immigrants and working mothers, and the other by contrast being a fairly 'well-to-do' rural town where many residents commuted to work elsewhere. The needs of the children in these two towns were therefore different, and it was possible to observe how programmes and activities were organized to suit children from either similar or different backgrounds and cultures.

The second comparative study was carried out in two districts of an industrial city. One district had an estate of privately-owned houses and a fairly mobile population which caused a high turn-over of pupils in the schools. The other district had a post-war housing estate, with seven tower blocks of flats and several two- and three-storey blocks; a large factory nearby provided employment for a number of people living in the district. Although an effort had been made voluntarily to supplement the generally poor amenities, this was still an area of social and cultural deprivation. A nursery centre, opened in 1974, gave care and early education side by side for a small proportion of children in the area. During this study, information was gathered not only on the variety of provision and organization but on the effects of educational policies and practices, such as age of entry to school and transfer arrangements, which differed from those found in the area of the first study.

A third study was made in an inner ring area of an industrial city and investigated how the authorities were cooperating to deal with the problem of trying to meet the need for care and education of young children. A nursery centre at the hub of the area supported by the education authority and social services was only able to take one-fifth of the children whose parents needed or wanted to use the centre. A number of other nurseries have since been opened as an extension of the centre and these are partly supported by funds from a charitable organization; the authorities have cooperated in an attempt to provide a comprehensive service for parents and young children. Three infant schools in the area, who received a number of children from the nursery centre, were visited so that forms of continuity or discontinuity could be observed.

In addition to the two nursery centres already mentioned a third one was visited. Each of these centres was quite unique in its structure and organization; two had a day nursery and a nursery class running side by side, the third combined these services as one nursery. All were jointly administered by the social services and education departments.

Visits were made to two infant schools with nursery classes in a county with widespread rural areas and several sizeable towns and cities. This county had developed a system for coordinating all the services for young children, which meant collaboration between education authorities, social services, area health services, playgroup association personnel, training establishments and local housing officials. Links had been formed which connected the complete range of provisions with each other, with their advisers and with their authorities. Visits to these two schools made it possible to see some of the effects of this system, and to discuss the benefits of a scheme which allowed teachers to be spared from their schools for up to half a day a week to visit and advise playgroups in their area.

Six outer London boroughs were selected for all other visits. In four of these boroughs, isolated visits were made to five schools with nursery classes or units and to two day nurseries. Observations were made in the reception classes and the nurseries. The organization of the day in each setting, the movement of children and staff, and the ways in which children were grouped, were particularly noted. From discussions with staff it was possible to gather information on arrangements made to effect a smooth transition for children moving into the school, either from the attached nurseries or from other provisions. In the other two selected boroughs a series of visits was carried out to observe the reception classes of four different schools. Each visit gave a picture of the sorts of experiences offered to the children on that day. By observing the same classes on several occasions it was possible to link the observations and see a progression of experience from 'settling in' to the introduction of more formal work.

These exploratory studies led to the identification of certain important issues which are discussed in the following section.

Identification of important issues

Factors which affect the amount and variety of provision

The need for care and education for pre-school children in modern society has already been mentioned in the introduction. At this point we are concerned with the provision available to parents for their children, and different factors which influence the amount and variety of this provision.

Regional or local differences must surely be one of the greatest influences on need and demand for provision. Rural and urban localities, for example, provide the greatest contrast of possible needs. Between the two come many variations. Density of population may be the first indicator of the *amount* of provision needed. The diversity of groups with different cultural backgrounds within the community of each area, the type of housing such as high-rise blocks of flats, and the availability of work for women may be indicators of the *variety* of provision needed.

It now seems to be recognized that while some mothers of young children of necessity go out to work to support themselves and their families, a growing number of others choose to work for reasons which arise from their own personal needs and domestic situation. 'Most employed mothers enjoy being at work and say they would choose to continue even if their family income increased – though some, especially among those in full-time jobs, say they would take the opportunity to reduce or alter the hours they work. They give a wide variety of reasons for wanting to go out to work, over and above money, and many of these reasons stem from the problems experienced by home-bound mothers.' (Hughes *et al.*, 1980.)

According to the Department of Employment *Gazette* (1977) the projection for employment rates for women with pre-school children in the mid-1970s in Britain was 18 per cent with a child aged nought to two years and 31 per cent with a child aged three to five years. This then forms one group of the population who need provision for their young children. A second group who also need provision are those parents, who, for various reasons, cannot provide adequate care for their children at home. These children will probably be referred by the social services to day nurseries, nursery schools or playgroups. Thirdly, there is quite a large group of parents who see part-time attendance at some form of pre-school as beneficial for their three- to five-year-old children, who can socialize and enjoy new experiences while at the same time the parents have some time free from child caring.

Mothers with babies and toddlers often need very flexible and temporary forms of provision or support which can be used in an emergency or for short periods. These may be especially needed by those who feel isolated without an extended family or friends in the neighbourhood and need the stimulation of meeting other mothers with their children. Discussions with advisers revealed that isolation tends to be the cause of problems particularly in rural areas. These problems may be aggravated by the closure of country schools and other services, and inadequate bus services and other forms of transport. The nature and effect of rural isolation on school entrants has not yet been adequately defined and assessed. Rural children are not exempt from some of the disadvantages which may be found in urban areas such as poor housing, insecurity, ill health, poverty, discomfort, and lack of varied experiences and opportunities for linguistic development. On the other hand, the needs of parents and young children in areas where the population is sparse are different from those in densely populated towns. In rural areas, facilities are likely to be a long distance away and small communities have to rely more on what they can provide for themselves, perhaps supplemented by services which are mobile and can come to them. Toy libraries, home–school link personnel, education advisers, playgroup advisers and sometimes health visitors try to mitigate isolation in some areas by making regular visits.

Local characteristics which influence the need and demand for preschool provision and other services will therefore have to be taken into account by the authorities when planning the variety of provision and services they consider appropriate for their area.

The amount and quality of provision and the level of activity between the education and social services authorities directed towards coordinating the services for the 'under-fives' will depend on the resources available. Where the amount and type of provision is inadequate to meet the needs of parents, other facilities will be sought and supplied by the private sector. Evidence was found of an increase in the number of childminders in areas where there were insufficient day nursery or full-time nursery school places. Also, insufficient nursery school and class places, whether full-time or part-time, had undoubtedly given good reason for the formation of playgroups to fill the gap.

The policies of local education authorities are another factor which affect the amount and variety of provision in each area. Policies regarding the age of school entry and frequency of admissions to infant or first schools, and policies which determine whether nursery places should be full-time, part-time or both, have considerable influence on the organization and content of early education in all sectors. Such policies differ from area to area. Recently many LEAs have admitted 'rising fives' to school. This has had the effect of reducing the age range of children in nurseries and playgroups of all kinds. However, some pre-school staff resented losing their top group of children; reception teachers were not always trained to deal with this age group and some schools did not have the appropriate staff, equipment or playspace for nursery age children. Frequency of intake is usually at the discretion of the head teacher, and arrangements for receiving new children are made accordingly.

There has now been a change of policy in some areas where the 'rising fives' are no longer admitted to school. Several places visited during the exploratory phase were in the process of gradually making this change. The effects of this will be felt throughout the range of provisions where adjustments to organization will have to be made.

Policies for full-time or part-time places in nurseries were influenced by the DES *Circular 2/73* which proposed that part-time nursery education should be made available for all children (between three and five) whose parents wished them to have it. The majority of nursery schools and classes have offered part-time places and held a few full-time places for children with special needs. Recently a few inner city areas have changed their policy to full-time provision and a few now offer an extended day, which would seem a realistic way of coming a step nearer to meeting particular needs.

Local authorities endeavour to coordinate the services for the 'under-fives' and make adequate provision for each area. Their efforts are often hampered by a lack of resources, which results in the fragmented development of provision in both public and private sectors. Although variety and flexibility may be desirable, many areas have difficulty in coordinating the total range of provision even when funds are used to employ personnel for this purpose. The aim to have adequate and suitable provision to meet the needs of parents and children everywhere still remains to be achieved in full.

Variety of types of provision

Responsibility in the public sector for providing care and early education is divided between the Department of Education and Science, and the Department of Health and Social Security. The division is basically clear cut in that schools, whether they be infant, first, primary or combined come under the local education authorities as do maintained nursery schools, classes and units. Day nurseries are run by the Department of Social Services who sometimes also take responsibility for foster-parenting services. In addition, this department takes partial responsibility in the private sector for playgroups, private nurseries including work-place crèches, and childminding. The social services require that these forms of provision should be registered with them and that the premises used should meet certain health and safety requirements. The number of children allowed to attend is also regulated by the social services.

At the local level the picture may become confused. Where coordination of these services has been attempted, the activities of both these authorities will be found to have extended, linked and crossed paths in a number of different and sometimes complex ways. For instance, the LEA may have appointed a teacher to liaise between playgroups and schools, to advise playgroup staff and help to run playgroup courses. A home-school link service run by teachers and nursery nurses may have been set up. Such services provided by education authorities were found to have widely different functions, although operating under the same name. In some LEAs, the responsibilities of the nursery and infant adviser were extended to include the playgroups; in others staff were appointed specifically to support both nurseries and playgroups.

The roles of personnel appointed by the social services varied. In many cases the same person was designated to support playgroups and child-minders, and such a person could be of considerable help in effecting the movement of children between minders and playgroups. In other cases, the support of playgroups, minders and day nurseries was combined in the appointment of persons with special responsibility for the under-fives. In these areas the day nurseries, who all too often work in isolation from other forms of provision, were more likely to be included in links with the schools.

In addition to these statutory forms of support from education and social services departments, there is a wide network of voluntary support, particularly in the form of playgroup advisers and fieldworkers organized by the Pre-School Playgroups Association. Both the statutory and voluntary bodies contribute to an extensive array of courses for parents and workers with young children.

These are just a few examples of the different forms of coordination which are known to exist and are fairly commonly found. Various other forms have been devised, many of which have developed over a period of time, and which may be dependent on funds being available to continue. Similarities may be found but the pattern of coordination will be different in each area.

Staffing ratios are considered an important issue when thinking of continuity for the child. All forms of pre-school care and education in Britain have a higher ratio of staff to children than schools do, so the new school entrant will inevitably have less adult attention available than before. The following were found to be fairly typical in the areas of the exploratory study: between 1 : 26 and 1 : 35 in reception classes; 1 : 11 in nursery classes/units/schools; between 1 : 4 or 1 : 5 in day nurseries; 1 : 3 (under-fives) in childminders' homes. Playgroups and other provisions in the private sector fluctuated around 1 : 6. These ratios sometimes varied from day to day depending on the presence of voluntary helpers and students.

During the exploratory phase a number of types and sub-types of provision were identified. These are described as follows:

SCHOOLS

In most cases the name of the school indicated the type of school and the age range of the children. Infant schools took children from five to seven years and first schools from five to eight or nine. There was a head teacher who took responsibility for the staff and the running of the school. Primary schools (infant and junior) took children from five to 11 and combined schools (first and middle) five to 11, 12 or 13. Larger schools had a head of the infant (or first) department as well as a school head; smaller schools were under one head. Where it was the policy of the local education authority to accept 'rising fives', there were a number of four-year-old children in the reception classes.

NURSERIES PROVIDED BY LOCAL EDUCATION AUTHORITIES

Nursery schools, nursery classes and nursery units were open during normal school terms for children from the age of three to five whose parents wished them to attend. There was usually a waiting list. In a few nursery schools, children of two years old were accepted. Morning and afternoon sessions of $2\frac{1}{2}$ hours each were usual. Regular attendance at one or the other of these sessions was known as part-time. Full-time children attended both sessions and had lunch at the nursery. Policies as to whether provision should be mainly for part-time or full-time education or a proportion of both varied from area to area, as did policies for providing extended nursery hours. The joint letter from the DHSS and DES of January 1978 states ... 'the overriding objective (of nursery education) is the child's linguistic, social, emotional, and physical development'.

Nursery schools were independent of infant schools and each was administered by a head teacher with a staff of nursery teachers and nursery nurses.

A nursery class or unit could be part of an infant, first, primary or combined school, but not all schools had one. It was administered by the head of the school and each unit or class had a teacher-in-charge.

A nursery class was accommodated in the main school building. Usually the staff of nursery teachers and NNEB-trained nursery nurses used the school staff room. School facilities, such as the hall, were often used by the nursery class at set times. Nursery class playspace was usually separated by a fence from the main school playground.

A nursery unit operated in the same way as a nursery class but was situated in a building separate from the school with separate playspace. The staff of the unit did not usually use the school staff room and often the nursery children did not use the main school facilities.

DAY NURSERIES PROVIDED BY LOCAL AUTHORITY SOCIAL SERVICES DEPARTMENTS

Day nurseries provided all-day care for children, usually between nought and four years old from 8 a.m. to 6 p.m. (these hours may vary slightly). Most children attended full-time, and day nurseries were open throughout the year except for bank holidays. 'Because of the limited number of places available in day nurseries priority for places is given to those with special need, including children of working lone parents, children with a mental or physical handicap, or whose home environment is so impoverished or so strained that they need day care, and those whose parents are, through illness or handicap, unable to look after them during the day.' (Joint letter, DHSS and DES, January 1978). The order given to these priorities was found to vary according to the most urgent need of parents and children in each locality. Families were often referred by health or social workers, and payment was on a means test basis. Day nurseries were run under the direction of a qualified officer-in-charge or matron and her deputy who were assisted by nursery nurses with NNEB qualifications.

PRIVATE DAY NURSERIES

These must be registered with the social services. They usually offered up to 8 to 10 hours of day care for eight or more children. No qualifications were required for the staff although they might be suitably qualified. Places were usually available to children whose parents were willing and able to pay the fees which could be quite substantial. Occasionally, fees were paid by the social services in a case of need. The premises used for private day nurseries varied from being a private home or a community hall to purpose-built accommodation.

Factory crèches were private day nurseries offering day care for children whose parents were working in the factory or one of the works in the near vicinity. The crèche was usually on the factory's premises and was often subsidized by the factory. A small fee was sometimes charged. Mothers were not generally encouraged to visit their children during working hours and did not participate in the running of the nursery. The adult-in-charge was usually suitably qualified.

PLAYGROUPS

There are various types of playgroup. All must be registered with the social services who control the number of children allowed to attend at one session and see that the premises meet the required standards for health and safety. The majority of groups are members of the Pre-School Playgroup Association (PPA). The premises used are usually the most suitable which can be found and vary from a church hall to purpose-built accommodation. Most playgroups provide part-time sessions only. Parents may choose the number of sessions per week that their children attend and pay fees accordingly. Part-time courses are available for playgroup leaders and helpers. The differences between the types of playgroup are often those of administration, organization and purpose. The following types were visited:

Community or committee playgroups were usually members of the PPA, and were run by a committee, largely comprised of parents of children in the group with one or two other interested persons, such as the vicar. Church halls were often used by these groups and usually only part-time sessions of six to 15 hours per week were offered. There was usually a permanent leader or leaders and a permanent second-in-command, who were each paid a small sum per session. Other helpers were usually mothers working on an unpaid rota system. Many leaders and helpers had attended courses run by the PPA for helpers and parents. These playgroups were non-profit-making, but small fees which varied from 5p to 50p per session were charged in order to cover running costs. The purpose of these groups was to provide children with the opportunity to play and socialize with other children, and to offer support for mothers and the opportunity to be involved and learn more about children.

Private playgroups, sometimes called nursery schools or kindergartens were run by private individuals, sometimes on a profit-making basis. They were usually members of PPA, partly to reap the benefit of discount on equipment and materials. Some private groups had been established for several years and used permanent premises; staff were engaged on a permanent footing although there could also be mother helpers. The fees charged were higher than for community or committee playgroups, and the permanent staff were marginally better paid. These playgroups provided part-time sessions only, but were usually open five days a week. Sessions were generally organized to a timetable.

Charity playgroups were those administered and run by a charity such as NSPCC or Save the Children Fund. They were usually situated in an area of disadvantage and run by people from outside the area. Parental involvement in these groups was less common although they could have mother helpers. Charity playgroups were often well-equipped and used good premises, such as the local health centre. They usually tried to give care and play experience to children who most needed it. Some operated as day nurseries, offering all-day care.

Local authority playgroups were administered and run by staff employed by the local authority. There were relatively very few of these, though some local authorities were known to sponsor a small number of places in the voluntary playgroups or to provide support in the form of low-cost premises, equipment loans or small grants.

Opportunity groups, usually set up voluntarily, were those which offered care and the opportunity for play and socialization to children with mental or physical handicaps as well as to normal children. These groups usually held part-time sessions with the choice of how many sessions per week a child might attend.

CHILDMINDERS

A childminder is required by law to register with her local department of social services to care for children in her own home for reward. She is allowed to care for a maximum of three children under the age of five, including her own 'under-fives'. She often provides this service for extended hours. The social services may provide advice, courses, and sometimes help with equipment. The purpose is usually to provide care for children during hours when parents are out at work. The parents' reason for using childminders was usually that no other provision was available which gave care during a full working day, though a few chose minders for preference. There were different reasons why childminders chose to care for other people's children. These reasons, which are mentioned under section (c) of this chapter, affected the aims of the individual minders. A fairly common aim was said to be 'to provide a home from home'.

Nursery centres have been set up in a number of inner city areas and densely populated localities. They are the joint responsibility of the education and social services authorities. The organization of these centres varied considerably. Many of them were running a day nursery providing all-day care for priority children side-by-side in the same building and sharing some facilities with a nursery class providing care and education with school hours and holidays. In a few of these centres the difficulties of having two authorities, two sets of working conditions, and different scales of pay for the same and nearly equivalent qualifications had been overcome. Only then could the centre really combine the services offered to parents and children.

The range of provision visited was extensive but not entirely comprehensive; mother-and-toddler groups and some of the less common types of provision such as playbus schemes were not included.

Variety within different types of provision

Here it is only possible to give some of the variations found within different types of provision. Those which have been identified as important issues are selected for brief discussion. As the project was concerned with looking at continuity of children's experiences, it was important to recognize some of the differences commonly found in similar types of provision and the reasons for these differences, which contribute to the diversity of individual experience but which may also be forms of discontinuity.

MATERIAL DIFFERENCES

The first obvious differences which may be found within all types of provision are the material ones of building, space and equipment. To some extent organization and planning of activities for children will be determined by the age and layout of the building and the space available both indoors and outside. Old school buildings usually have spacious rooms but movement is restricted by walls and doors. As teachers cannot keep an eye on children outside the room, activities are usually confined to the classroom unless the teacher has ancillary or parent help. Modern open-plan schools may actually have less space per child but allow more freedom of movement for staff and children, and therefore require a different type of organization which may involve different grouping of children and perhaps team teaching. The picture is similar for all types of provision, but the advantages or disadvantages of an old or modern building may be different. For instance, a few nursery schools are still housed in temporary war-time accommodation with a series of small rooms while new nurseries are usually built to an open-plan design. Teachers said that as small children like and feel more secure in small rooms and cosy corners, the old buildings had some advantages. Corners usually had to be created in the open-plan nurseries.

The amount and quality of equipment found in different provisions of the same type varied and was related to the length of time the provision had been established, the amount of funds available and the ideas, theories and resourcefulness of the adults concerned. Sand, water, dough or clay, painting materials and crayons were usually considered the basic materials for encouraging the development of skills and concepts in young children. These were found in most reception classes and in various forms of pre-school provision but not in all. A few schools believed that children had already experienced sand, water and dough, and now they needed the stimulus of different materials. Usually, however, sand and water for play in the reception class were intended to provide a form of continuity for children already familiar with them and a new experience for the few who had not used them before. All nursery schools and classes were found to have these materials. Day nurseries and playgroups of all types usually had them, while childminders seldom provided for messy activities with sand, water or paint in their own homes; play with water and earth was sometimes allowed in the garden.

The way in which equipment was used or allowed to be used varied within provisions of all types. The options might be: free choice for the child from all the available equipment; limited choice from what was made available; adult-directed choice (e.g. would you like to play Lotto?) or no choice at all. The training and philosophies of the adults concerned, the needs of each particular group of children, the space available, the daily routine, and possibly parents' expectations could all play a part in determining which of these practices were adopted.

Outdoor facilities were provided for all infant schools, nursery schools and classes, and day nurseries. The former might have no large play-ground equipment, while nurseries were usually well-equipped with large fixed equipment such as climbing frames and a quantity of smaller equipment like wheeled toys, rockers and balls which were brought out of store daily. Playgroups and other provisions in the private sector often had no outdoor play facilities. If their indoor space was large enough, attempts were usually made to compensate by providing some large equipment indoors and by allowing children plenty of gross physical movement. Groups using church halls quite commonly did this.

Organizational differences within provisions may be very slight or may be important issues. The age range of the children accepted, the hours during which a provision is open and whether staff are working a shift system as in day nurseries, are basic to the organization of each provision and may differ only slightly within the different types of provision.

Methods of grouping children, teaching styles, 'ground rules' (meaning what is expected of the child), constraints, and organizations for playtime and mealtimes are among the important issues which affect the child and may provide continuity or discontinuity of experiences.

Within infant and first schools, different types of grouping were found. Children might be grouped horizontally by age, so that there were separate classes for five-year-old, six-year-old and seven-year-old children. Or the school might be vertically grouped, with the children in each class representing the age range of the school; this method of grouping is sometimes referred to as 'family grouping'. Some schools used a combination of these two forms of grouping. They were generally known as semi-vertically grouped schools: either some children were grouped into classes representing more than one year age range, or all the children were organized into groups representing the total age range of the school for some activities only. Grouping arrangements were often changed from year to year as considered appropriate for the children on the roll and the new intake.

Teachers usually adjusted their methods and teaching styles to suit the age range and the particular children in their class. Most teachers organized their classes into smaller groups. They then had to find ways of dividing their attention between their pupils, either by moving around to attend to groups and individuals, or by remaining in one place while the children brought their work to them. A consequence of both strategies was that some children inevitably had to wait for attention. (See Chapter 5 for examples of this.)

Arrangements for playtime and mealtimes in schools, particularly for new entrants, varied considerably. Staff of some infant and first schools were aware of the differences that children coming from pre-school or home had to face in terms of greater numbers, noise, and constraints on time and duration of play, and made arrangements to introduce children gradually to these changes (see Chapters 9 and 10).

AIMS

Within the different types of pre-school provision the variations in ground rules, adult expectations, choice of activity and parent participation are usually related to the individual philosophies and aims of staff in charge. In broad terms each type of provision has the common aim of providing care, or care and education, and some also include support for parents. These aims are usually made more explicit by the adult in charge of each type of provision, who may also place emphasis on certain aspects.

Schools and nurseries under the education authorities understandably placed emphasis on education and child development. The care which young children need became an integral part of early education. The amount of parent participation or involvement varied from school to school and nursery to nursery. While the primary aim of day nurseries run by the social services was to provide care for priority case children, and usually support and help for their families, some day nurseries were deliberately introducing an educational element. Policies and aims within different day nurseries were found to vary. Some saw themselves as providing care for as long as it was needed, probably until the child went to school. Others saw themselves as a short-term solution for children and parents where there was a priority need; when and if circumstances changed, children could be returned to normal family life and attend nursery school or playgroup.

Playgroups varied more in their aims for parents than for children. Playgroups who were members of the Pre-school Playgroups Association tended to set great store on parent involvement, but all thought that providing opportunities for children to play and mix with peer groups was their main purpose.

Individual childminders had different reasons for choosing to care for other people's children. It was found that the childminders visited were either working on a temporary and intermittent basis or they regarded their work as a profession. The reasons they gave for becoming child-minders were that while staying at home to look after their own child they might as well mind another one or two as company for their own and to make a little money; or that their own children were all at school and they missed having a child in the house; or they just preferred to work at home rather than go out to work. Their expressed aims varied from looking after the child while mother was at work, to providing a home from home and being a substitute mother. One of these childminders was actively involved with a playgroup, and encouraged her own and minded children to indulge in all the messy activities while at playgroup. Few childminders were found whose expressed aims included providing opportunities for play experience to encourage the development of early skills and language, although one working on a professional basis had conscientiously set out to teach a child to talk.

Where common aims were found, these must surely form a basis for continuity of experiences for the child. Widely differing aims and adult expectations may cause discontinuities in the child's experience.

COMMUNICATIONS

Communications between people involved in the care and education of young children was expected to be important in establishing continuity, so information on existing forms of communication was sought in the areas explored at this stage. Communications in most of these areas were found to be rather limited and often confined to those between schools and their attached nursery classes or units and sometimes neighbouring playgroups. In each area it was found that children visited their first school at least once before entry. The extent to which teachers and other adults who were receiving new children were aware of each child's previous experiences varied considerably. The tendency was for the minimum amount of information, or no information at all, to be passed from one provision to another. Parents were often asked to give brief details of their children's previous experience when completing school admission forms, so teachers usually knew whether a new child had come from home or had attended one of the local pre-schools.

Teachers seldom knew much about any of these pre-schools, unless it was the nursery class or unit attached to their own school. They had rarely had any contact with local playgroups, day nurseries or childminders. Several reception teachers commented that they recognized different types of behaviour in new entrants as indicative of children's previous experiences. Noisy behaviour and failure to respond to adult directions except when spoken to as an individual, might be taken as indications that the child had been used to complete freedom of choice and movement and was unaccustomed to being one of a small group. More controlled behaviour might be expected of children coming from a place where the organization of the day imposed some limitations on choice and movement and where there was more adult direction.

In the areas where links and cooperation existed between schools and the other settings, it was found that adults working with groups of children who would soon be going to school were helping to prepare these children for transition by introducing them to more structured activities and helping them to build more realistic expectations of school.

The majority of areas visited during the exploratory study lacked a system of communications which linked all forms of pre-school provision and infant schools. Some links were found but rarely did these form a complete circuit of communications between all the adults who were concerned with the care and education of young children. Therefore attempts to provide forms of continuity were often confined to small pockets within the community rather than being the general pattern.

The exchange of information between parents and forms of provision tended to be the minimum considered necessary. There were pre-schools who aimed to develop relationships with parents, particularly day nurseries who tried to provide family support and playgroups who involved mothers as helpers. Yet while they did not underestimate the importance of the family, they did not always see a need to cooperate with other provisions in order to give continuity for children moving to a new setting. The knowledge that parents might provide the most important means of continuity often appeared to be overlooked when links were being forged and communications developed.

By the end of the exploratory phase, a number of issues had emerged which clearly could have a crucial effect on the experiences of young children. These were:

- regional and local variations in the amount of pre-school provision

- the variety of types of provision

- the local authority policies on admission and transfer

- coordination of services and communication between provisions

- differences between and within types of provision in terms of:
  - perceived aims and functions
  - physical settings, facilities and equipment
  - staffing ratios
  - adult styles of working with children
  - organizational differences: ages of children, hours of attendance, grouping, meals and playtime
  - activities available and constraints upon their use
  - communications with parents

These issues delineated the areas of inquiry for the research and with these in mind the team began planning strategies and methods of investigation.

CHAPTER 3

The Research Studies

In order to research the issues which had crystallized from the exploratory phase, two levels of inquiry were distinguished: firstly, the *general* level, which would yield a description of the variety of provision available; secondly, the *particular* level, which would examine the individual experiences of children as they made the transition from home or pre-school provision to infant school.

The first would be an extensive study, taking a *cross-sectional* view across the range of infant and pre-school provision in selected areas. The second would be an intensive study, taking a *longitudinal* view of a sample of children about to start school. The research was thus divided into two parts: the cross-sectional study and the longitudinal study.

The cross-sectional study

In order to describe the variety of provision available to children between three and eight years of age, the team needed to explore the following questions:

How do children spend their time in the different provisions? What activities do they engage in? Does the range of activities, and children's participation in them, differ according to the type of provision or the number of adults available?

How much choice do children have in what they do? Is the degree of choice related to the type of provision, the type of activity or the organization of the group?

To what extent are adults involved with the children? Does involvement vary with the type of provision, the type of activity or the number of adults available?

How are the children grouped: how much do they work or play alone, in
groups or as a whole unit? What is the age range of the group?
What equipment and facilities are available to children? Are these related
to the type of provision and whether it is voluntary or state supported?
What are the policies and procedures for effecting children's transition to
school?
How much liaison is there between the various provisions and what form
does this take? Is any information about children passed on from one
provision to another?
What aims and expectations do staff have for the children?
What are the patterns and extent of parent involvement?

To find out the answers to these questions, the team needed a design
which would be flexible enough to capture the variety and fluidity of
provisions catering for young children. Two methods were chosen: direct
observation in natural settings, supplemented by contextual information;
and face-to-face interviews with staff.

The observation instruments

1. The scan: in each provision the children were observed for a two-hour
period which was timed to include activity time. At five-minute intervals
the observer scanned the area of observation (the room, the garden, or
both if both were available to the children) and wrote down what everyone
was doing i.e. the activities in progress and the number of children and
adults at each. The observer sought to record as accurately as possible
what children were actually doing, rather than the equipment they were
using e.g. 'trickling sand through the fingers' instead of 'at the sand tray'.
2. The mode: throughout the same two-hour period of observation, the
observer continuously monitored the mode of operation i.e. the constraints which influenced the children's activities in terms of the degree
of choice they had, the way they were grouped and the involvement of
adults with them. Any changes in choice, grouping or adult involvement
were noted.
3. Details of environment: for each provision the observer completed a
schedule noting details about the building: its age, size and design;
facilities and amenities; children's furniture; storage; pictures and displays; and outdoor playspace.
4. Equipment checklist: a checklist of more than 150 items was used to

record what materials each provision had and whether they were available for the children's use.

The interviews

The adult responsible for each provision was interviewed about the numbers and ages of the children and hours of attendance; fees and grants; staff roles, qualifications, and their aims and expectations for the children; organization and grouping; pattern of the day, special activities and outings; liaison with other provisions and the recording and exchange of information. Six interview schedules were designed so that appropriate questions could be asked of childminder, officer-in-charge of a day nursery, playgroup supervisor, nursery teacher or head, infant teacher, and infant school head.   All the instruments were developed and refined over a series of trials. Inter-observer reliability was between 70 per cent and 100 per cent. The instruments finally used owe much to discussions with Corrine Hutt at Keele and the early work of the Oxford Preschool Research Group.

In order to carry out the fieldwork, the three members of the research team separately visited sample schools and pre-schools including the homes of childminders. Each visit lasted a day. If the observation took place in the morning, checklists and interviews were completed in the afternoon. This pattern could be reversed in all-day provisions in order to balance the number of morning and afternoon observations.

The sample

In selecting the provisions to be visited, two criteria had to be borne in mind: firstly, regional and local variations in what was available; secondly, the variety of different types of provision.

Seven local authorities were selected whose populations ranged from urban and immigrant to rural and overspill, and which, according to their rating on clusters of social indicators (DHSS, 1977), represented a variety of need. Three were London boroughs and four non-metropolitan counties.

Six types of provision were identified: childminders, day nurseries, playgroups, nursery schools, nursery classes or units, and infant classes. The sample was balanced so that half the provisions were in the education sector and half were in the social services and voluntary sectors. Provisions in each area were selected randomly within the types available there; the number of each sub-type (private, community, local authority etc.) reflected the proportions which existed in those areas.

The final sample of 181 provisions was made up as follows:

63 infant and first classes: these were vertically, semi-vertically and horizontally grouped and spanned the range of five- to seven- or eight-year-olds.

28 nursery education provisions: i.e. 12 nursery units, nine nursery classes and seven nursery schools.

41 playgroups: i.e. 24 private playgroups, 15 community or committee playgroups, two local authority playgroups.

22 day nurseries: i.e. 16 local authority, five private, one charity-supported nursery.

27 childminders: i.e. 14 with, and 13 without, under-fives of their own.

The findings

The information gathered from this study is used to describe where and how children spend their time. Similarities and differences among the provisions are revealed and give an indication of how much children's experiences are likely to be interrupted in moving from one kind of provision to another. The findings provide a background to the second part of the research: the longitudinal study.

The longitudinal study

Through this study, the researchers sought to establish a rich profile of individual children's experiences over a period of several months around transition to infant school, and to study the responses of the children and their parents to this change. The following questions were explored:

In what ways do children's experiences change as they move from home or pre-school provision to infant school?

How do children respond to these changes? What things stay the same?

Does the child's experience before and after starting school differ with regard to activity, choice, adult involvement and attention, or social behaviour?

Are any observed differences related to other changes in the child's experience, such as size of group or provision, ratio of adults available, physical setting, patterns of attendance, adults' ways of working with children, and contact with parents?

Does the child's response vary according to pre-school experience, age at entry to school, admission policy and procedures, the preparedness of child and school, availability of information for parents and staff, liaison between provisions, parent and staff attitudes and expectations, or the presence of siblings?

What differences do children and parents experience when children start school? What changes occur at home and does the child's behaviour at home alter?

To discover the answers to these questions, the researchers required a strategy which focused on the individual child and his view of the world as he made his passage from pre-school into school. To this end, the team adopted the case-study approach by which a detailed description of each child's experiences and responses was built up. Again, two methods were used: direct observation of the child in his school and pre-school settings; and loosely structured face-to-face interviews with staff and parents before and after the child's transition.

The observations

Each child was observed during his last six weeks at home or pre-school and his first six weeks at infant school. He was observed during the last two hours of the morning session (or before lunch) and the first two hours of the afternoon session (or after lunch). Children attending pre-school provisions for half days only were observed half as much as those attending pre-schools full time. The child was observed for ten minutes in each hour once a week. Thus in six weeks the whole of a two-hour span was covered. Throughout these observations, the observer noted where the child was, how many children and staff were there, what the child was doing, the degree of choice and direction, whether he was working alone or with others, and what adult attention he received; incidents of non-compliant behaviour and details of any interactions with adults were also noted. Inter-observer agreement was between 75 per cent and 98 per cent.

In addition to these systematic observations, informal observations were made of the child's behaviour and response to routines such as arrival and departure, dinnertime, playtime and assembly; and to adult-led sessions for PE, music and movement, television, story and news.

The interviews

The child's parents, the adult in charge of his pre-school, the head of his infant school and his class teacher were all interviewed in this study. The purpose of the interviews was to obtain relevant information which was not available to the observer's eye.

Pre-school staff were interviewed before the child started school, infant staff after his first month at school, and parents both before and after the transition. Staff were asked about their provision's organization and procedures; their own attitudes to schools, pre-schools and transition; their contact with other provisions attended by the child, and their expectations of him. Parents were asked about the child's home behaviour; their attitudes to and contacts with school and pre-school; their aspirations for and expectations of their child; and his readiness for and adjustment to starting school. Parents were interviewed on both occasions in their homes.

The sample

The study was conducted in two phases: the first phase concerned a sample of 21 children starting school in September; the second a sample of 15 children starting school in January. The sample included one child who did not attend any pre-school provision and two children who were attending more than one pre-school concurrently.

The 36 target children were selected in four different local authorities. Three of these had been sampled in the cross-sectional study, but the scope of the research was extended to different provisons. The areas were urban and multi-racial, suburban and semi-rural. During the study, one of the children moved into a fifth area which was rural. The sample, though small, was sufficiently diverse to embrace a variety of pre-school provision and transition procedures; infant schools both large and small with new and existing reception classes; and a range of social and cultural backgrounds. Criteria for selection were that the children should represent as wide a variety of provision as possible and that for practical reasons they had a good record of attendance. Permission was sought from education and social services departments, staff and parents. Clusters of infant schools with their neighbourhood pre-schools were sampled. Children were randomly selected from transfer lists; they included pupils transferring from the same pre-schools to different schools, and from different pre-schools to the same school. The total sample was made up as follows:

11 children from two nursery units
three children from one nursery school
13 children from seven playgroups
six children from three day nurseries
one child from a playgroup and childminder
one child from a playgroup and nursery unit
one child from home

The 36 children transferred to 12 different infant schools. Their ages when they started school ranged from four years four months to five years four months. There were 19 boys and 17 girls.

The findings

This study yielded a series of rich descriptions of the experiences of individual children before and after transfer to school. These highlight the continuities, discontinuities and sources of distress encountered by new entrants. Their individual experiences can be viewed against the broader background of results from the cross-sectional study.

The findings of both studies are reported in the following chapters. Towards the end, three case studies are included to give the reader a flavour of the complexity of influences which impinge on the young child and which interact to make his progress more or less smooth.

But we cannot see inside a child's mind to know what it is really like for him. The findings rest solely on what the researcher was able to observe and what was reported to her. Indeed, the observer herself, while remaining as neutral and unobtrusive as possible, may have been an instrument of continuity as the children were followed from pre-school into school. Nonetheless, within the limits of the sample and the methods at their disposal, the researchers have sought to identify some of the critical features of continuity in early education and care, and to suggest practical guidelines for easing transition.

Note

A complete set of observation and interview schedules are available for perusal in the library, NFER, The Mere, Upton Park, Slough, Berks.

CHAPTER 4

School and Pre-school Settings

Children coming into infant school around the age of five bring a variety of experiences with them. Many of them have already spent time away from home in playgroups, in nurseries or with minders. The child who has been in a day nursery from babyhood will have spent most of his waking life during the past four years away from home; another child may have spent no more than two or three hours a week away at playgroup. Some have sampled a succession of different provisions, starting perhaps with a minder and moving later on to nursery. Others may have attended more than one concurrently, spending most of the day with a minder who took them to playgroup for a couple of hours or attending a playgroup in the mornings and a nursery class in the afternoons. Only a very small number of children may have come to school straight from home. It follows then that the new entrants being welcomed by their reception teacher on their first morning at school represent a potentially immense diversity, each one arriving with his own particular history of pre-school experience.

So what is it like for these new arrivals? What differences do they encounter as they move into infant school and what things stay the same for them? How do they respond to the changes they experience? To answer these questions we need to look in detail at what children do both before and after transition to school: how they spend their time, where and with whom. These are discussed in the following three chapters.

Settings

The place in which a child spends his time away from home becomes his physical world for the time he is there. It provides the setting for his activities, and what he does will be influenced or constrained to some extent by the place he is in. So before we can adequately describe children's activities we must first examine the environments in which they are carried out.

Childminders' homes

The homes of childminders are as various as homes generally. We visited 27 minders in inner-urban, suburban and semi-rural areas whose dwellings dated from pre-war to new and ranged from houses which were terraced, semi-detached and detached to flats in low and high rise blocks. Their gardens were similarly diverse, each house having a small or medium-size plot in which the children could play. Most were securely fenced, though one or two on open-plan estates presented problems of safety and supervision. Many of the gardens contained both grass and hard surfaces for play and were pleasant with trees and flowers. Three minders provided the children with a patch of their own to tend. Very few were fortunate enough to have a covered area, a boon with lively youngsters in wet weather. Fixed apparatus for outdoor use is expensive to buy and only three or four swings, climbing frames, sandpits and paddling pools were observed. The children in upper floor flats of course did not have direct access to outdoor playspace other than balconies and walkways which required constant supervision. This meant that these minders could not with peace of mind allow their charges outside, but had to take them to the play area at the foot of the block or to the local park if there was one.

One in three minders allowed their charges to play with toys belonging to their own offspring but this can have drawbacks for the family. Older children who are away at school may resent their belongings being used in their absence, so their bedrooms were often out-of-bounds to young visitors. In fact, very few minders permitted the free run of the whole house, restricting the youngsters to a limited number of rooms or the downstairs. If the minded child's toys are to be kept separate, storage can be a problem. Makeshift containers, particularly cardboard boxes, were in frequent use but bookcases and garden sheds were not usually accessible to the children. In three or four homes nursery pictures and pieces of the children's work were displayed on the walls, and nearly half the minders provided at least one child-size table or chair in addition to use of the larger furniture.

Playgroups

The 41 playgroups we visited were housed in a variety of buildings, none of which had been constructed for the purpose. Three were held in leaders' own homes which in each case was a detached house. The rest made use of premises belonging to other organizations. These were all single-storey buildings ranging from pre-war to almost new. There were church halls, village halls, community centres, sports pavilions, cricket clubs and the headquarters of scouts, guides, first aiders and the mentally handicapped. Three groups operated on school sites, in spare classrooms or in rooms available for community use. Buildings varied tremendously in size and appearance from pre-fabs, Nissen huts and Terrapins to more permanent constructions of brick and stone. Most playgroups functioned in one hall-like room with toilets, kitchen and occasionally a smaller room adjoining. Some premises were drab and draughty, others light and airy, but most were a challenge to staff who wanted to create a cosy, attractive setting. Dusty floorboards need frequent sweeping or covering with rugs, while polished floors have to be protected from scratches and spills. High ceilings can cause echoing and heat loss. Large areas must be broken up by playcorners, screens or makeshift boundaries of chairs if noise and running about are to be minimized. Rooms which are used by other organizations cannot be freely adorned with the children's work, nor can play equipment be left out. At the end of the session the room must be cleared and swept clean ready for the next user.

The display of pictures and children's art work on the walls was evident in only eleven playgroups, usually because to do so was impractical, impossible or not allowed. A few leaders improvised with screens which could be packed away after use.

Most of the playgroups had child-size tables and chairs, but the seven who had none made do with whatever furniture was available, such as trestle tables and full-size chairs. Child's height toilets, washbasins and coatpegs were rarely seen.

Storage often taxed the ingenuity of staff who were constrained to stow equipment of all shapes and sizes under the stage or in an inadequate cupboard out at the back. In all cases such store places were not accessible to the children to help themselves. The ubiquitous cardboard box proved indispensable for smaller items as did the use of laundry baskets and washing-up bowls. More than half the groups had bookracks for the children's use.

Outdoor toys presented a real headache since few groups possessed an outside store. More important, eleven had no suitable outdoor playspace at all. Among those who had, there was an enormous variety of car parks, fields and gardens. Only one had a covered area for wet weather use. Very few owned climbing frames and sandpits, though some luckier groups were sited in public parks with swings and roundabouts nearby. Because of inadequate outdoor facilities and the effort involved in making them safe, many playgroups abandoned outdoor play entirely in the winter months.

Day nurseries

The 22 day nurseries in our sample differed from the playgroups in most cases by having exclusive use of the premises they were in. This has important implications for the facilities at the children's disposal. Activities and displays do not have to be put away every day but can become ongoing or semi-permanent parts of the environment. Amenities and furniture can be tailored to suit a specific age group and outdoor play space can be equipped with fixed apparatus.

Our day nurseries comprised thirteen specially built for the purpose, either the prefabricated war-time type or modern single-storey units; three converted from their original designs; and six in halls and houses. In all cases children's work was displayed on the walls and there was an adequate supply of small tables and chairs. Unlike the playgroups, most nurseries provided each child with his own peg on which to hang his coat on arrival, and in a few he also had a drawer or cubby-hole in which to keep personal possessions.

All the nurseries had outdoor play space which was easily accessible and securely fenced. Most had both hard and grassed areas and more than half had a covered patio and a garden shed for toys. Trees and shrubs were much in evidence, and one private nursery garden was specially designed to provide interesting nooks and crannies for young explorers. Fixed apparatus like swings, climbing frames, logs and stepping stones were seen in most nursery gardens.

The nurseries on the whole were better off for storage than the playgroups and a range of cupboards, trolleys, bookshelves and boxes was in use.

Nursery schools

In the field of nursery education we visited 28 provisions and seven of these were nursery schools. Only two had been purpose-built; the rest had been adapted for nursery use. There was the rambling old house hung with virginia creeper; the mossy war-time prefab; the red brick Victorian school; the attractive blue and white bungalow. Like the day nurseries they all had exclusive use of the premises. Moreover, every one of the schools comprised more than one room. Indeed one school occupied two buildings which were separated by a garden, public footpath and playground, so for most of the time they functioned as self-contained units with the head teacher commuting between them.

All the schools were well-equipped with suitable furniture and facilities, and there was a fair variety of storage space. Every child had his own coat-peg which he identified by the small picture beneath it. Children's creative work embellished the walls and table displays flourished everywhere.

Like the day nurseries, the schools had ample outdoor playspace in the form of interesting gardens or imaginative playgrounds. These all contained fixed apparatus varying in kind from caravans and log cabins to concrete tunnels and old boats.

Nursery classes and units

Many infant, first and primary schools provide for under-fives by having a nursery class or unit. We defined a 'unit' as having its own self-contained building distinct from the rest of the school and we sampled twelve of these. They were all single-storey constructions and most of them had been built in recent years, being favoured by some local authorities as successors to the more traditional nursery school. Almost all of them were purpose-built and differed from the nursery schools by being open-plan inside, comprising a large playroom with smaller quiet areas and story corners around the edge. Only one differed by consisting of two classrooms in an annexe formerly used by infants.

The nursery classes, of which we visited nine, were contained within the main school buildings and occupied rooms which had been either specially constructed for them or adapted from existing classrooms. They tended to be smaller than the units but usually had access to other parts of the school like the hall and the use of school equipment such as PE apparatus, record players, television and reference books.

Like the day nurseries and nursery schools, all the classes and units were furnished with small tables and chairs, a variety of storage space and a personal coatpeg for every child. Pictures and displays abounded everywhere creating bright attractive interiors.

Every class and unit had its own outside play area, though this could vary from a fenced garden used exclusively by the nursery children to a section of the main playground available only when the rest of the school were indoors.

It will be apparent from these descriptions that pre-infant school settings are many and varied, ranging from the comparatively small and compact world of private homes to single big playrooms or halls, and rooms which are components of larger institutions. But what of the infant schools into which the children eventually have to come? What are they like?

Schools

We visited a total of 43 different schools which represented the entire range from infant or first schools to combined infant and junior or first and middle schools. Since many of these also had nursery classes or units and occasionally playgroups and toddlers' clubs on the same site, it was possible for some pupils to come into contact with children as young as three or less and as old as eleven or twelve. Some schools also contained a special unit for children with learning difficulties or physical disabilities. One exceptional campus contained a first, a middle and a high school; a playgroup; and a building for general community use, so that in effect it catered for the entire age range of the local population.

School premises vary enormously and those we visited encompassed old and new and consisted of single or multiple buildings, some with an upper storey. Designs have changed over the years and layout is usually a clue to age. In earlier years there was a tendency to construct chains of box-like classrooms. These might stretch in a long line with a corridor running the entire length or be arranged around open quadrangles. Both designs could be built with an upper storey and we encountered schools like these in urban areas, often with the junior department upstairs and the infants on the ground floor. A variation of this is the 'finger' plan, where three or four short lines of classrooms extend like fingers from the hall and administration area. More recently, buildings became more open inside and classroom chains with corridors gave way to paired rooms with shared activity areas arranged in clusters around a hall. Many suburban schools are variations on this theme. There are, of course, schools which defy classification or are combinations of the designs which have been described.

Infant classes

The 63 infant classes we visited were distributed throughout the range of buildings already described. Three-quarters of them were enclosed like boxes and the rest were open- or semi-open plan. However, the word 'open' is probably a misnomer since very few classroom areas are open on all sides and in most cases teachers made use of folding doors, curtains and cupboards to form screens and space-dividers. Where pupil numbers had exceeded designers' intentions, the use of activity areas as classrooms resulted in further limitations of space.

The majority of infant classes share at least some resources with the rest of the school and this extends their territory and gives them access to a wider range of materials than their base room can offer. The hall for instance is used for assembly, film shows, talks; displays of work; and activites like physical education, drama and music. In many cases it also doubles as a dining room: less than a third of our sample had a separate room for school meals. Most schools also had a library from which the children could borrow books to take home, though it was not always available to the reception and nursery children. About a third of our classes had access to a resource area containing special activities like weaving, printing and pottery, and a few schools with high immigrant populations managed to set aside a room specifically for the teaching of English as a second language. Nine of our infant classes were situated away from the main school, usually in terrapins across the playground, but occasionally a reception class was housed separately rather like a nursery unit.

Since almost all the classrooms were used exclusively by infants, a wealth of material could proliferate and unfinished projects remain undisturbed till the following day or week. Furniture and activities were rarely static and teachers frequently changed them around to stimulate fresh interest. A room could develop from being rather bare at the beginning of term into a richly decorated treasure trove of paintings, models and table displays. By the end of the term, especially at Christmas, rooms were transformed into Aladdin's caves of shining mobiles and glittering collages.

At infant school there seems to be a greater emphasis on personal territory than in the pre-schools. Children tend to have a fixed work base which usually means sitting at a certain table or block of tables for more formal tasks like writing and number work. In many cases children have their own particular place at the table. If they move away to paint at an easel or listen to a story in the book corner, they have a place to return to at certain times of the day. Some teachers let their pupils sit wherever they choose, but most of them allocate each one a drawer for books, papers and crayons, and a coatpeg not only for outer clothing but also for shoe bag and PE kit.

Storage takes many forms and there is a great deal to be stored, so our classrooms contained a variety of cupboards, walk-in stores, bookshelves, trolleys and boxes. Nests of drawers were very prevalent and were indispensable not only for children's personal use but also for a myriad small items like beads, counters, coins, mosaics and puzzles. Open shelves and the tops of low cupboards were also utilized to the full and had to be kept tidy, as almost everything except stock cupboards was accessible to the children at some time.

Very few schools, though, owned an outside store and portable equipment for the playground usually had to be carried from the hall. All our classes had access to a playground but a third of them had to share with children in the junior department or the nursery, though not usually at the same time. Playgrounds varied considerably in size and shape from rectangles of bald asphalt to landscaped areas with grass and trees. Paths were often lined with shrubs or flowers and occasionally a pond, fountain or dovecote provided added interest. Most play areas were relatively large, sometimes comprising an adventure area or a playing field and four had a swimming pool for summer use. Yet only half were securely fenced all round which meant that staff had to be particularly watchful.

Scale, range and movement

From these descriptions of school and pre-school settings, it is evident that there is considerable diversity, not only between the different types of provision but also among them. No two are quite alike. The multifarious nature of children's learning environments therefore makes it difficult at first to see any strands of continuity between them. Clearly the transitions from one to another are as idiosyncratic as the children who make them. Yet there are certain aspects common to all of them which are worth further consideration. These are: the *scale* of the child's setting, the *range* of his territory, and the limitations on his *movements* within it. The significance of these is perhaps best illustrated by the actual experiences of individual children.

Eric settled into school so well that he surprised his parents who were expecting a tearful start. He came from a nursery unit attached to another school. His new class was a reception unit set apart from the main school. The two units were similar in several respects: they were both modern buildings, each comprising a large open-plan playroom with its own outdoor play area; each was self-contained with its own toilets, handbasins and coatpegs. The nursery unit had a quiet room for stories and discussions, the reception unit a similar room for television and music. At nursery Eric had made a fortnightly trip to the main school hall for assembly. In his new school he also visited the hall for PE and hymn practice, but these were introduced gradually till after several weeks he went nearly every day. At playtimes Eric went out to the main school playground but again this was introduced gradually and at first his class went out to play before the rest of the school so that they had a chance to try out some of the adventure equipment there. Dinners would also be eaten in the main building but not until the second week when he would stay at school all day.

So for Eric the change of school was in many ways a transfer between two very similar settings. The scale of his physical world within the unit remained virtually unaltered, and the range of his territory beyond this familiar base was extended only gradually. These undoubtedly contributed to his air of cheerful confidence in the early weeks.

It seems logical to suppose that environmental changes are minimal for the child who transfers from a nursery class to an infant class in the same school. He will be familiar with the building and the approach to it, and will know some of the children and staff. The nursery class has probably been included in the school assembly and also invited to the hall for special occasions like concerts and plays. They may also have used the hall for physical activities and had access to other rooms for books and television. But the integration of the nursery class into the rest of the school depends upon school organization and staff attitudes. In some cases lip service only is paid to the notion of inclusion and a nursery class may be no more a part of the school than a nursery unit across the playground. If the nursery class is sited at one end of the corridor, it is possible for the young child to be in a self-contained world. If he also comes and goes through a separate door he may be scarcely aware of the bigger world of school that lies beyond his own room.

The discontinuity for the child, whether he comes from the nursery class down the corridor or the playgroup down the road, is surely the extended range of his territory when he comes to school. Plan 1 illustrates the range of Kim's territory in her wooden hut playgroup and then in her infant school. Notice the contrast as Kim moves from the limited range of a single playroom with car park to a paired classroom with open shared areas. Her new class works in team with the class next door, sharing three rooms between them for most of the day. Kim goes to a fourth area for phonic work and to the hall for PE, movement, assembly and dinner. At playtime she uses the full extent of the spacious irregular shaped playground and part of the playing field beyond.

But discontinuities like these are not necessarily disadvantageous for the child. Kim settled happily at school and clearly was ready for the stimulus which the transition offered. Her formerly characteristic pose of standing sucking two fingers was rarely seen after starting school.

On the other hand, however ready she is for change, the child may not be able to cope if the discontinuities are too extreme. Plan 2 illustrates the experience of Sundar who left the compact world of a small open-plan day nursery for a large rambling school built in the classroom chain and corridor style. Facilities were so dispersed that he had to make many long and tedious expeditions in a day. At day nursery he often looked bored but the much-needed change, when it came, was so great that throughout the early weeks he frequently looked lost and bewildered.

Not only had the range of Sundar's territory been considerably enlarged but his movement was constrained in a way he found uncongenial. For several years he had been used to roaming freely throughout the rooms of the nursery and the garden outside more or less as and when he pleased. At school he was confined to one rather crowded box-like classroom which he might leave only at appointed times and in a certain manner. Because facilities were so far apart he had to walk in lines with his classmates to toilets, television room, language room, library, dining room, hall and playgrounds. At the same time as his territory had been extended his movement around it had been severely curtailed.

Restrictions on movement within the base itself may also be a discontinuity. Ian attended a playgroup in a spacious community hall where an uninterrupted expanse of floor gave him ample opportunity for riding round and round in his favourite pedal car. He transferred to a crowded classroom of children aged five to eight where movement around the room

Plan 1: The range of Kim's territory at playgroup and school

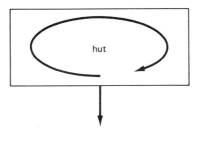

hut

car park

Playgroup in single-room hut

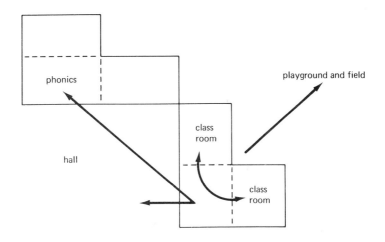

phonics

playground and field

class
room

hall

class
room

Infant school with paired classrooms and shared areas

Plan 2: The range of Sundar's territory at nursery and school

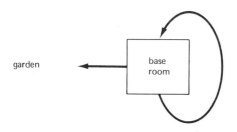

Compact open-plan day nursery

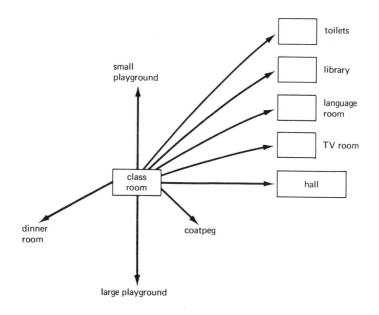

Large infant school with long corridors and dispersed facilities

was impractical. Ian found it impossible to sit still. He coped by creating a thousand excuses for leaving his seat and frequently left the room for the toilets. His teacher coped by placing him at a table by himself where he would not disturb others and allowed him free access to her desk without having to wait his turn.

The experiences of these four children enable us to see how transitions between quite different environmental settings may be made more or less congenial. For Eric his bases in nursery and reception unit were similar in size and scale. The extension of his range to strange territory beyond was a gradual process, whereas Sundar was compelled from the start to make long excursions in order to reach toilets and play areas.

Kim's transition was between two very different settings: the playgroup hall and the semi-open-plan infant school. But here again there was continuity of scale within the base setting. The hall was well-equipped with child-size tables and chairs, the large floor space broken up by play corners, and the careful use of screens and cushions provided cosy retreats from the hurly burly. The three areas which formed her base at school were colourful and interesting, with nooks for quieter pursuits and ample opportunity for her favourite activity of make-believe play.

What distinguished this from Sundar's school was the design of the building. This was his first encounter with closed box-like rooms and long corridors. Unlike Kim, he was confined to one room instead of three and facilities were a long way off while hers were close at hand. The consequent restrictions on his movements imposed by both dispersed facilities and a small enclosed classroom were further discontinuities in his experience. Like Ian, he suffered from the sudden curtailment of the comparative freedom enjoyed at pre-school. For Kim and Eric, changes in scale and movement were slight, extensions to their range were introduced gradually, and they settled easily. But Sundar and Ian encountered sudden considerable changes in scale, range and movement and they both had difficulty adjusting to them.

Change is inevitable and people have to make the best use of the buildings they are in. But the transition between different settings is made smoother for the child if the following ingredients are present:

- a secure base of appropriate scale. If we kneel down we get some idea of the relative hugeness of our surroundings from a child's eye view. Small-size furniture, low-level displays and pictures on eye-level all help to create a child-oriented setting.

- a gradual extension of the range of new territory. Extending a child's range gives him scope for moving away from the base. At school the introduction to new and exciting areas beyond the classroom can be a stimulating experience, but needs to be a gradual process if the child is not be overwhelmed.

- the careful organization of space to the young child's needs. Neither the confines of a congested classroom nor the uninterrupted freedom of a large playroom are desirable, but rather a distribution of space which allows for movement without disrupting others. This means breaking up space to create corners for privacy and quiet as well as open areas for movement and activity. The child requires a setting that allows for both noise and quiet in activities and for both freedom and control of movement.

- familiarity with the school before he starts will give the child an idea of what to expect and may help him cope more easily with change.

CHAPTER 5

Activities

The activities children engage in depend not only on the setting they are in but also on the equipment available for their use. This in turn is related to what the staff are trying to do for the children in their care and the resources they have with which to do it. However, it is important to remember that the aims people express and the resources they have can vary considerably from place to place; the findings discussed below give a picture which is typical of the sample but which may not necessarily be the case everywhere.

Staff aims and goals

We interviewed minders and the staff of each pre-school provision about their aims for the children and the role they thought their particular establishment performed. The minders emphasized basic care and security: 'I try to make it like being with mother, make them feel happy and safe'. This sentiment was echoed by the officers in charge of day nurseries who felt they were also providing a community service and giving support to parents in need.

The care and support function of childminders and day nurseries contrasts sharply with the chief aims expressed by playgroup leaders and nursery teachers. Both felt they gave the children experience in mixing and sharing, opportunities for learning, and a sound basis for starting school. They felt basic skills were important and by the time each child left he should be able to recognize his own name, know simple numbers and be able to use a pencil, paintbrush and scissors.

In nursery schools the accent was on the individual, and head teachers felt they should try to develop each child's potential and meet each child's needs. By the time he transferred to infant school he should be able to communicate fluently. Both nursery school and day nursery staff wanted the children to become self-confident and able to get on with others. But the over-riding goal in all types of provision was independence: that by the time he went to school each child should be able to dress and feed himself, cope with the toilet and look after his own belongings.

The provisions are united, then, in their chief goal of child independence but differ in what they perceive their main function to be. This, together with the different financial resources at their disposal, has repercussions on what they provide for the children to do.

Equipment and materials

The potential range of equipment is enormous; we isolated 150 categories on our checklist. If we look for items which are most commonly in use we find our sample provisions group like this:

> childminders
> local authority day nurseries
> nursery schools, classes, units and committee playgroups
> infant classes

Childminders

The minded-child's environment is seen as a temporary substitute for home and usually contains the stuff that family homes are made of: television, story books, soft toys and dolls, model cars, crayons, tricycles and trucks. These vary in quantity and condition but form the basic ingredients of most minders' homes. In addition, things like shape boxes, toy telephones, small bricks, and a musical instrument to bang or blow are fairly common. We found that materials for creative work were very limited, consisting mainly of paper and paints and occasionally plasticine or dough. Surprisingly, there seemed to be a dearth of pencils and children sometimes took a fancy to the researcher's. Most minders said they did not mind messy activities but of course these are not always easy to accommodate and were rarely in progress when the observer called. A few minders, however, did allow children to stand on a chair at the sink or use the bath for waterplay.

Minders are rarely paid enough to allow them to spend money on expensive toys. In some areas toy libraries exist which operate a lending service; however, very few of our minders availed themselves of this facility even if they knew of it. They all took the children out regularly though, mostly to the shops, the park or the local playgroup.

Here is a typical day in the life of a minded four-year-old:

8.00   arrives at minder's house, plays while minder's family get ready for school.

9.15   plays or 'helps' minder with chores: washing-up, dusting.

10.45   has a drink and a biscuit; listens to a story or watches television.

Twice a week goes to playgroup for the morning.

12.30   lunch and sometimes a sleep.

2.00   is taken out to shops, park or to visit friends.

4.00   watches television; has drink and snack; plays with minder's children who have come home from school.

5.30   goes home.

Day nurseries

The day nurseries try to create a homely atmosphere by organizing the children into small groups with their own nursery nurses and their own room. The children may spend most of the day in this room or use it as a base to return to for stories, rests and meals. The room usually contains a 'home' corner for domestic play, soft toys, books and a range of puzzles and construction toys. The private nurseries in our sample varied considerably in the amount and condition of their equipment; this probably reflects the fact that they operate on a fee-paying basis, the amount charged being arbitrary. On the other hand the local authority day nurseries, which are administered by the social services, were comparatively well-equipped indoors and out, especially those which had been purpose-built. Items which were in use in most day nurseries included: pedal toys, prams, rockers, barrels and tyres; floor layouts, small bricks, Lego, jigsaws and pegboards. Pets were usually kept, and most nurseries owned a record player and some a television set too.

Materials of a creative nature were usually put out selectively, different ones on different days: painting and printing things, glue and scissors, plasticine and dough. Sand was available in half the nurseries but water-play was less often available. Pencils were not usually used.

Here is an example of a child's day in a nursery:

8.00	arrives at the nursery; equipment for the morning's activities is put out.
9.00	breakfast; group discussion time: news and chat.
9.30	choice of activities indoors (and out if fine).
11.45	dinner; rest-time; older children can play quietly and talk in whispers.
2.00	choice of activities.
3.00	tea; listens to a story.
4.00	plays or watches television.
5.00	goes home.

Nursery schools, units, classes and playgroups

In accordance with the tenets of nursery education, there are certain elements which form the staple props of every nursery school, class and unit. Each has its book corner, home corner, dressing-up clothes, sand and water, paints and brushes, floor toys and climbing frame. These cater for the intellectual, imaginative, creative and physical aspects of the child's development. In our sample they were echoed in the playgroups, particularly the committee ones. Private playgroups, like the private day nurseries, were more variable and just as there were those which were well-equipped, there were others where materials were sparse and in poor condition. All playgroups operate on a shoestring, but the shoestring may be lengthened or shortened by various means. All of them rely for their income chiefly on the fees they charge which are relatively small. Committee playgroups are non-profit-making and recruit parent helpers who give their services for nothing or next to nothing. Income is used for maintaining and equipping the groups and usually has to be supplemented by fund-raising events. The owners of private playgroups, on the other hand, operate in several ways. They usually employ regular staff at a fixed wage. Some make no profit at all and even subsidize the group from their own pocket. Others run them like a business, sometimes having a chain of playgroups in one area and circulating equipment among them.

Considering the different ways in which they are financed, it is amazing that some playgroups have managed to emulate the equipment of nursery schools and classes. In the state education sector the head teacher is given a requisition allowance for each child. The money is allocated under certain categories such as furniture, books, and indoor and outdoor play materials. The teacher's training helps her to judge how best to spend the money and which materials to choose. Playgroup equipment, on the other hand, depends on the amount of income available, the rules and regulations of the premises, the willingness of the leader to spend profits and her knowledge of the children's needs.

The child who attends a nursery school, class, unit or playgroup can expect to meet a certain range of items, though these will vary in quantity from place to place. He will find toys to pedal, push and rock; model farms, zoos and garages; construction kits like large Lego; bricks, pegboards, shape boxes and beads; Fuzzyfelts, jigsaws and picture boards; sand and waterplay. He will have opportunities to use scissors and glue, crayons, paint and dough.

But our nursery schools and classes also provided things of a more permanent nature which playgroups in borrowed premises could not do so easily, such as interest tables, quiet corners and areas for specific activities. (See Plans 3 and 4.) They had better facilities for doing woodwork and cooking. And they were better equipped to fulfil their stated aim of 'giving practice in the basic skills' with a more plentiful supply of pencils, picture lotto, dominoes and sets for sorting, matching and shape recognition.

For the child who attends nursery or playgroup the morning goes something like this:

9.30   arrival; choice of activities indoors and later outdoors as well if fine.
10.30   drink and biscuit; registration and discussion.
11.00   choice of activities.
11.45   clearing up; stories, rhymes and music.
12.00   goes home.

The programme in most provisions is a variation on this theme, free play being interspersed with periodic reassembly of the whole group. Starting and finishing times may be earlier than in the example and in some provisions the session lasts three hours. There may be children who stay all day, particularly in nursery schools, and they have dinner sometimes followed by a rest. The afternoon programme is usually similar to the morning.

Plan 3: A hall playgroup with no outdoor playspace

This is a plan of one playgroup we observed.

Activities are set out for the morning session. To compensate for the lack of outdoor playspace, part of the floor area is set aside for physical activities. Compare this with the plan of a purpose-built nursery unit.

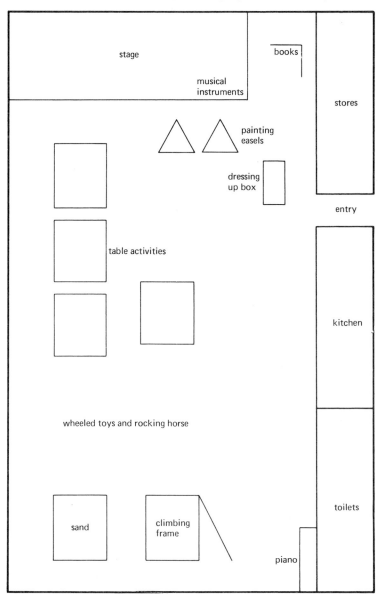

Plan 4: A purpose-built nursery unit

This is a plan of one nursery unit we observed.

Notice the extensive range of equipment, particularly the more permanent features like special areas and play corners.

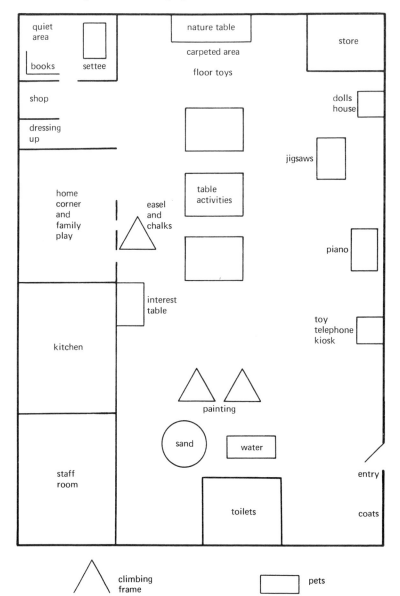

The pre-schools, then, provide a diversity of settings in which the child is weaned away from his mother and encouraged to develop into a confident and sociable person. The distinction between care and education is a blurred one: both are provided in some measure, the different emphases being reflected in what is available for the children to do. Materially, an increased awareness of *all* aspects of the child's development is manifested in the purchase of equipment which encourages muscular coordination, cognitive and manipulative skills, and creative and imaginative expression.

The infant class

On entering an infant school we find that many of the familiar objects of the pre-school are there, but a closer look reveals a gradual thinning-out as we move up the school and a noticeable shift in emphasis from some types of equipment to others.

The precise nature of classroom materials is largely determined by the age-range of the pupils. The new entrant may come into a reception class in which all the children are around five like himself; or he may enter a mixed age group of five- and six-year-olds; or if the school is vertically grouped, his companions can be up to eight or nine years old. Where younger children are present there is likely to be a greater distribution of typically pre-infant equipment. For example, a reception class usually contains at least some of the basic elements of nursery education described above such as a home corner or Wendy house, a book corner, a carpeted area for floor toys and, less commonly, trays for sand and water. (See Plan 5.) A mixed-age group requires a more extensive range of equipment to cater for different abilities. This means that unless space is plentiful the amount of 'younger child' equipment has to be limited to allow room for 'older child' materials and access to it is curtailed by organizational constraints.

Certain materials common to most pre-schools are found in many classrooms particularly those geared to younger infants: bricks, and construction sets of plastic and wood; floor layouts, and models of cars, animals, people; pegboards and bead-threading; music-making instruments like shakers, drums, tambourines and triangles. Here too is the creative area with paints and brushes, a supply of junk and collage materials, glue and scissors. Familiar sheets of computer print supplement the stock of sugar paper which provides colourful backgrounds for art work.

Plan 5: A reception classroom in a primary school

This is a plan of one reception class we observed.

Compare this room with the playgroup and nursery unit. Notice the elements which are common to all of them, and those specific to the primary school: maths corner, phonics table, and the seating arrangement.

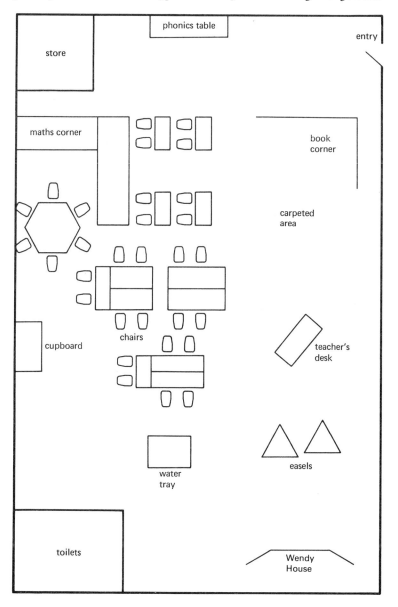

But infant classrooms also contain much that is new and unexplored to stimulate inquiring minds and busy fingers. In the book corner nursery rhymes and picture books give way to well-illustrated reference books as well as stories. There are fewer play corners for fantasy and dressing-up but more interest tables with collections of objects for natural science or ongoing projects. A 'maths corner' displays apparatus for counting, weighing, measuring. Materials abound for matching, sorting and word-recognition. Boxes hold dominoes, draughts, chess and jigsaws of increased complexity. Sand and water are used less for tactile experience than to demonstrate concepts of volume and capacity. Charts and pictures are integrated with children's work to adorn the walls and audiovisual aids such as television, tape recorders and record players are frequently used.

The chief tools of every infant are probably his pencil, exercise books and crayons, which together with his reading book make up the scholastic contents of his drawer. Most schools implement a reading scheme, a carefully graded series of books through which the child's progress is monitored step by step.

The shift away from pre-school materials is perhaps nowhere more obvious than in the apparatus used to develop physical skills. Gone are the toys to pedal, push or pull, and the slides, swings and rockers. Instead, the infant is more likely to be using balls and beanbags, hoops and skipping ropes. Many school halls are equipped as gymnasia with wall bars, parallel bars, window ladders, climbing ropes, vaulting boxes, forms and mats.

The child at infant school is surrounded by a rich variety of apparatus and equipment, probably greater in quantity and diversity than he has ever encountered before. But for him the biggest discontinuity from pre-school is their limited availability; he may explore them only at certain times. A glance at this typical pattern of an infant's day tells us why this is so:

9.00	arrival and registration
9.15	assembly in hall
9.45	number work; milktime
10.25	playtime
10.40	reading, writing and English work
12.00	dinner and playtime
1.30	art and craft activities

2.40   playtime
2.55   story
3.15   goes home

This example demonstrates the segmented nature of the infant's day. Time is divided into periods of prescribed activity. There are disruptions for specific events such as PE (physical education), music, and hymn practice for which the hall is used at certain times. There are fixtures like 'assembly' when classes meet for worship (described in Chapter 8) and 'playtime' which occupies natural breaks in the programme (see Chapter 9). The rest of the time consists of three main blocks of classroom activity delineated here into numeracy (number skills), literacy (reading, writing and language skills) and creativity (art and crafts). There are of course variations on this basic pattern: in some schools all or some types of activity may be going on at the same time, but most commonly the more formal reading, writing and number tasks are done in the morning and the messier activities in the afternoon.

The infant school pattern has two important consequences for the child transferring from pre-school. First, access to the wealth of material around him is restricted. He is expected to do certain things at certain times thus precluding the use of equipment not relevant to the tasks in hand. If he is supposed to be completing a writing task, he cannot be building Meccano or playing at the sand tray; physical education apparatus is available only during his PE period. At pre-school he could usually choose freely from the range of activities set out for the session; there might have been one activity he was expected to take part in, like making a Christmas card or a Halloween mask, but even this was not compulsory. At school he can choose freely at certain times, usually when he has finished prescribed tasks. This brings us to the second consequence of the infant school pattern: the explicit distinction between 'work' and 'play'.

Nursery education is traditionally oriented towards play. Freely chosen and self-directed play is the chief means by which children learn; they play, but they play with a purpose. At primary school the notions of 'work' and 'play' are distinguished. There are set periods called 'playtime' and periods for doing number 'work' or English 'work'. Exercise books are called 'workbooks' and the phrases 'Get on with your work' and 'I've finished my work' are commonly heard.

The distinction between work and play is more than a semantic one. Children are allowed to play in the classroom as a reward for finishing their work: 'you can choose something to play with now' .... 'can I play with the sand?' The notion of work offers a stimulus to those who want praise or personal success. It is occasionally used at pre-school with the 'rising fives' to make them feel more grown-up: 'Would you like to come and do some work at the big table?' Many children respond enthusiastically to the idea of doing 'real work' when they get to school and want to start straightaway. Like Debbie, the twin in Chapter 11, they are thrilled to be given a workbook and pencil on the first day. Of course, not all children view work as a status symbol. Ian's efforts were so messy that he could not aspire to the dizzy heights of an exercise book and had to do everything on paper at first. Some teachers allow such children to 'play a lot till they are ready'.

Equipment and materials play an important role in the transition of the young child as he moves into infant school. The gradual change in *content* simultaneously ensures:

- familiarity with a modicum of items previously encountered in the pre-school

- the stimulus of an expanded range of new and exciting materials

The change in attitude towards their *use* results in:

- restricted access imposed by the daily pattern

- the explicit distinction between work and play

What activities do children engage in?

A description of equipment and materials tells us nothing about what the children actually do with them. We therefore tried to focus our observations on the precise activity the children were engaged in rather than on what they were playing with. This enabled us to look for strands of continuity in what children do in the different provisions. For example, it is not enough to know that a child is at the sand tray. We need to know what he is doing there: trickling sand through his fingers; running toy cars along a sand track; seeing how many small containers can be filled from a large one; or simply gazing into space. These are four quite different activities and it was important to devise a way of dealing with such differences.

Accordingly, when the fieldwork was finished, we grouped all the activities we had observed under broad headings. These are elaborated below to give the reader an idea of the enormous variety of activities in which young children engage.

First, activities concerned with the acquisition of skills:

Gross Motor

Activities which promote coordination of the large muscles. These include body movements like running, hopping, crawling and whirling around; repetitive movements like rocking, bouncing and swinging on a swing; pushing, pulling, riding and pedalling toys; playing with balls; throwing and tossing hoops and beanbags; rolling barrels and tyres; climbing, sliding, balancing and hanging on equipment; and games like ring-of-roses and follow-the-leader.

Spatial, Perceptual and Fine Motor

Activities which promote perceptual skills, spatial orientation or fine motor coordination. The child may be visually sorting or matching colours and shapes; involved in understanding size, distance, angle and perspective as when building dens, constructing with small blocks, fitting, stacking, hammering and threading; or using materials requiring perceptual and fine motor coordination such as puzzles, shape boxes, Lego, Meccano and scissors.

Artistic and Tactile activities

The child is using two- and three-dimensional materials to express himself or further his tactile experience. He may be drawing, painting and printing; doing junk modelling or collage; moulding pliant substances like clay, plasticine and dough; and playing with natural substances like water, sand, soil or salt.

Musical activities

Those which promote expression through rhythm, movement and sound. The child may be dancing or moving freely to music, listening to sounds, chanting or singing, and using rhythmic patterns with musical instruments or hand clapping.

Imaginative and Representational activities

The main focus is on developing the imagination or creating representational settings. The child may be pretending to be someone else like Batman or a Dalek; assuming a role as in family play; or using models and scale toys like farms, zoos, cars and dolls.

Verbal and Symbolic

Activities which promote verbal skills such as speaking, listening, reading and writing; use language to establish meaning; and use language, symbols or structured material to foster the development of mathematical and abstract concepts. The child may be counting, weighing, measuring, calculating; naming letters, copying words, writing sentences; looking at a book, watching television, listening to a story; discussing news; or listening to instructions and explanations.

Understanding the Physical World

The child is exploring the properties of the physical world and living things: examining plants, insects, flowers; watching birds, fish, pets; planting bulbs and seeds; experimenting with objects which sink, float, dissolve and melt; or investigating reflections, magnets and batteries.

Next, activities which are concerned with the child's basic care and the organization of his programme:

Activity Preparation and Termination

Getting materials out, putting on an apron; clearing up and putting away; showing work to adult.

Domestic Routine and Physical Care

Toilet, washing and dressing; eating and drinking; resting and sleeping; having first aid; registration; organized movement to and from base.

There are those behaviours which indicate the child is not involved actively in anything, such as:

Waiting

Lining up, queueing, waiting for teacher or for an activity to start.

Watching

Looking on at other people or activities without being involved.

Cruising

Wandering around, gazing into space, or other non-specific behaviour.

Finally, emotional and social behaviour which is not embedded in other activities:

Social Expression: neutral or positive

The child may be simply engaged in social contact; expressing positive feelings of affection, pleasure, joy; or making gestures of kindness like helping or comforting.

Social Expression: negative

The child is expressing genuine negative feelings like anger, fear or hostility; or engaging in negative behaviour like aggression, tantrums or destructiveness.

These categories embrace just about everything we saw children doing in their schools and pre-schools. We can use the categories to compare and contrast what children were doing in the various types of provision.

Activities in pre-schools

A profile of how the children spent their time is given in Table 1 (p. 63). It is based on data gathered in the first (cross-sectional) study. In each provision a whole class or group was observed for two hours. Every five minutes the observer scanned the group and noted what all the children were doing. When the group became absorbed into a larger mass, as they did in playtime or assembly, this was noted separately as a special 'time-tabled' period. These occurred in infant schools rather than pre-schools.

The profiles of nursery schools, classes and units were so alike that they can be considered together. Furthermore, their joint profile is remarkably similar to that of the playgroups. This means that children attending playgroups were spending their time in much the same way as those going to nursery schools, classes and units. This general resemblance between playgroups and nursery educational provisions accords with the similarity we have already seen in their stated aims, range of equipment and sessional pattern. In all these groups the same three types of activity predominated, occupying more than half the children's time. These were: spatial, perceptual and fine motor activities; art and tactile activities; and imaginative and representational activities. The groups differed, however, in the fourth major area, gross motor play. The playgroup children did less of this, which is understandable when we remember that outdoor playspace was often limited or non-existent.

These same top four types of activity predominated in the day nurseries too, but to a lesser extent since more time was taken up with domestic routines, clearing away and cruising. Compared with their peers in nursery education and playgroups these children did fewer of the imaginative, creative and fine motor activities but exceeded everyone else by spending a fifth of their time in gross motor play. This is probably a direct reflection of the materials at their disposal since the day nurseries were comparatively well-equipped with outdoor play areas, large apparatus and wheeled toys but had fewer play corners, creative materials and table toys.

Since the same four types of activity claim so much of the pre-school child's time we are prompted to ask why this is so. Is it a matter of children's preferences that they spend their time in the way they do? The Oxford Preschool Research Group (Bruner, 1980) reported a preponderance of large scale motor, manipulation, construction, art and pretend play in their observations of nursery schools, classes and playgroups. And a Canadian team (Morgan *et al.*, 1979) studying the characteristics of kindergarten children aged four to six found that 'the preferred activities of children were in the gross motor, language and creative areas'. This team also noted the low incidence of environmental study and science, a finding echoed in our own observations of 'understanding the physical world'. In Canada, as here, the approach is one which allows children to make choices. But ultimately choice must depend on materials: a child cannot choose what is not there. Perhaps the higher incidence of cruising among day nursery and minded children reflects the fact that they do not have enough of what they would like to play with. The crucial role of materials becomes clear if we take a closer look at the main activities.

Gross motor

Children in nursery education were more inclined to be climbing, sliding and swinging on large apparatus whereas playgroup children rode around on wheeled toys. Day nursery children did a lot of both, but minded children relied more on their own body movements without apparatus.

Spatial, perceptual and fine motor

Predominantly using construction sets, except in nursery classes and units where manipulative activities like bead-threading, pegboards, stacking, screwing and nesting took precedence.

Art and tactile

Particularly sandplay, except in playgroups and minders' homes where painting or colouring were favoured more.

Imaginative and representational

Children in nursery education played more with scale toys like layouts and model farms or zoos. In playgroups and day nurseries the accent was on family play, while mindedchildren played with toy cars or indulged in fantasy.

Mindedchildren spend their time quite differently from those attending the voluntary and state provisions. Equipment-oriented activities occupy a much smaller proportion of the day; instead there is more emphasis on behaviours which are part of home life, like eating, drinking, washing or doing nothing in particular. This tendency is reflected to a lesser extent in the other full-time provisions and is a natural consequence of a programme which must cater for all-day needs.

How the pre-school child spends his time, then, is largely a consequence of the interplay between a provision's aims, functions and resources. Will he spend it any differently when he gets to school?

Activities in infant schools

From observations in infant classes we constructed a profile of activities which is shown in Table 1.

It is tempting to assume that infant classes form a homogeneous group but this is not so. The observed sample covered the entire age range from five to eight. Depending on the organization of the school the youngest and oldest children in a class could be from six months to three years apart. This can fluctuate from year to year depending on intake numbers, staffing quotas, space available and so on. Because of the almost infinite variations in age composition we found it impossible to group the classes in any meaningful way for comparison. The profile therefore comprises the whole infant age range but is nonetheless useful in highlighting the kind of activity-world our new entrant is moving into.

The profile for infant classes is indeed different from the rest. The four types of activity which took precedence in the pre-schools are no longer prominent in the infant day. Gross motor activity is mainly confined to timetabled periods of PE in the hall and to playtime outside. The daily programme allows fewer opportunities for art and tactile expression: drawing and colouring still have a place particularly in conjunction with written work which children are encouraged to brighten with their own illustrations, but access to painting, collage and clay is limited, and sand- and waterplay fade out of the curriculum. Imaginative expression becomes minimal, consisting of domestic role play rather than fantasy and scale models rather than dolls. Perceptual activities like sorting, matching and ordering still feature in the child's programme, but construction sets get smaller demanding finer motor control, and manipulative tasks like threading, stacking, screwing and hammering almost disappear. The whole balance of the child's curriculum has swung away from these activities to those of the verbal and symbolic kind or, more colloquially, the 3 Rs. We found that children in infant classes were engaged more often in verbal and symbolic tasks than in any other type; in fact these

Table 1: Activities: Profile of activities engaged in by children in 181 schools and pre-schools (as a percentage of times observed).

ACTIVITY	Infant classes (63)	Nursery schools, classes & units (28)	Play-groups (41)	Day nurseries (22)	Child-minders (27)
Gross motor	1.3	17.3	13.5	20.3	9.6
Spatial, perceptual and fine motor	10.1	16.4	16.7	12.7	9.2
Art and tactile	8.1	17.0	16.9	12.3	8.8
Musical	1.9	2.6	2.5	1.8	1.2
Imaginative and representational	3.5	16.3	16.6	13.2	22.5
Verbal and symbolic	32.4	7.2	8.6	6.4	7.8
Understanding the physical world	.3	.5	.6	.9	.4
Activity preparation and termination	9.0	4.2	3.3	5.2	4.9
Domestic routine	8.2	7.0	6.9	8.4	13.5
Waiting	9.3	1.6	3.6	3.9	1.0
Watching	.1	.3	.8	.6	2.0
Cruising	8.0	7.6	7.4	9.9	14.1
Social expression (neutral/positive)	.3	.7	1.0	1.2	1.4
Social expression (negative)	—	—	.1	.1	.4
Timetabled periods (playtime, assembly)	5.4	.1	—	—	—
Not assigned	2.1	1.2	1.5	3.1	3.2
%	100	100	100	100	100

accounted for a third of all infant activities. For the pre-school child this type of activity consists mostly of looking at books and listening to stories. The infant does these too but also participates in the whole range of literacy and numeracy tasks: learning to recognize sounds and figures; tracing, copying and writing letters, patterns, words and sentences; making up stories and telling news; answering questions and following instructions. He grapples with mathematical concepts by using coins and clocks, weighing shells and cones, measuring hands and feet, calculating with coloured rods and beads. Most of all he practises language, reading and number skills in written exercises using work cards and text books. These may be part of a published work scheme such as 'Fletcher maths' or supplementary material made by the teacher.

We found that infants, like pre-schoolers, engaged least in activities to do with understanding the physical world. Musical expression was also low in the activity league everywhere; brief bursts of rhyme-singing and clapping could happen almost daily in group sessions, but opportunities to move to music or play percussion instruments only occurred once or twice a week. This was particularly true of schools where a class might go to the hall at appointed times for radio programmes or hymn practice.

We observed infants getting out materials and clearing them away twice as often as pre-schoolers. There are three reasons for this. Firstly, the older child is more capable of organizing what he needs and there are fewer adults available to do it for him. Secondly, the schoolchild is usually given a personal supply of books, pencils and crayons which he keeps in his own drawer and gets out when required. Thirdly, the proximity of purpose-built storage items like low cupboards, shelves and trolleys makes them easily accessible to youngsters. In the pre-schools, activities are usually set out by the adult at the beginning of each session, changed around halfway through and cleared away at the end. Where possible children are encouraged to help tidy up but it is not always practical for them to put equipment away. For playgroups in particular, unsuitable premises can mean storage space is out of children's reach and even dangerous. In many a rented hall which has to be stripped of all trace at the end of every session, the children help carry toys to one end and leave the grownups to do the heavier work of folding and stacking.

Perhaps the most striking difference between pre-schools and infant classes in general is in the amount of 'dead' or non-task time. Infants did at least three times as much waiting, queueing and lining-up as pre-schoolers. Together with cruising and other non-specific behaviour this amounted to more than 17 per cent of all infant activity. This marked

increase in dead time is largely a consequence of organizational procedures. These are brought about by three factors:

1. the presence of large numbers of children who have to compete for
   resources by taking turns or waiting for a place e.g. queueing for
   dinner or a turn on the climbing frame;
2. the design of the building and dispersal of facilities which necessitate
   the supervised orderly movement of children to and fro e.g. lining
   up to go to assembly, and
3. the ratio of children to adults which means competition for the
   teacher's attention e.g. waiting to have work checked.

In the pre-schools there were usually about five or six children for every
adult present. At school there are likely to be as many as 20 or 30. The
infant teacher is faced with the task of dividing herself among them as
efficiently as possible and this has implications for the way she organizes
her class. There are two popular alternatives: either the children remain
in their places and the teacher moves around the room to each child or
group giving help where needed; or the teacher remains in one place and
the children come to her when they require attention.

Here is an example of each taken from observer's notes:

In Nadia's class
afternoon activities are in progress. The room contains 18 children all
in their first term at school. Nadia is absorbed in tracing the outline of
a cat. When she has finished she looks around for Miss Lewis who is
busy with a group doing potato prints. Nadia wants to know what to do
next but cannot catch the teacher's eye. She calls 'Teecha, Teecha'
three times. Miss Lewis says 'Just a minute Nadia'. Nadia swings back
and forth on her chair sucking her pencil. A minute later her teacher
comes over. They discuss the picture and Miss Lewis explains how to
go on. Nadia picks up a stubby wax crayon and is soon absorbed in
colouring the cat blue. She takes the finished tracing to Miss Lewis
who is talking to children at the Wendy house and waves it under her
nose. At first the teacher ignores her, then acknowledges her efforts
with a brief 'Good girl' and says 'Now you can play in the playhouse if
you like'.

In Melanie's class
there are 31 children aged five to eight. The first activity period of the

morning is in progress and children are seated at their tables doing English work tasks. Melanie has drawn a picture and waits for her teacher to write a sentence beneath it for her to copy. Mrs Perry sits at her desk in one corner of the room and Melanie is eleventh in the queue. She chats and laughs with the girl next to her. A boy starts pushing and the queue collapses noisily. After five minutes it is Melanie's turn. She dictates her sentence and Mrs Perry writes it down: 'I played with my sister on Saturday and Sunday'. Melanie makes her way back to her seat to finish her work. By this time the queue stretches as far as her table and she cannot pull her chair out to sit down. She waits good-naturedly for two more minutes, then copies the sentence quickly with the queue still pushing around her.

The success of both methods depends on the kinds of activities in progress, the range of the children's ages and abilities and the skill of the teacher. Neither method is foolproof. Moreover, these examples present a cogent argument for smaller classes or higher adult ratios.

Activities around five

What we have described so far is a general picture of the activities of children from three to five at pre-schools and from five to eight at school. We have noted the marked swing in the balance of the curriculum from one stage to the next. But for the child actually making the transfer around the age of five the changes may be a good deal less drastic. The experiences of our 36 target children highlight what can happen around the time of transition.

Each child was observed for ten-minute periods throughout his last six weeks at pre-school and first six weeks at school. Profiles derived from these observations are given in Table A, Appendix. While the experiences of this small sample are essentially idiosyncratic, they do serve to illustrate several important points about children starting school.

Our target children in nursery education and playgroups did more activities of the verbal and symbolic type than their younger companions, though the same was not true for the minded and day nursery children. There appeared to be a conscious effort on the part of some pre-school staff, as there was with the home child's mother, to prepare these children in some measure for school. Here is an observation of Pippa in her nursery unit:

Pippa was playing by herself, wheeling the pram with the doll she had just tucked in, when the teacher invited her to join a group playing a game of Lotto with plastic animals. The teacher leads the game asking 'Who has an elephant? Who has a green seal?' The object of the game is to identify the animals and to learn their names and colours. Pippa joins in with evident enjoyment, interacting verbally with teacher and group.

On the other hand, the rising-five-year-old may of his own accord be more specific in what he chooses to do. Here is Tamsin in her last two weeks at playgroup:

She has just put the finishing touches to her second painting containing a spider, the sun and several wigwams on a strip of green. She goes alone to a table and sets out a number card game. She points to the picture of milk bottles on one of the cards and counts them aloud to herself from one to ten.

Reception teachers usually help to ease the passage of new entrants by allowing them more flexibility than older pupils, neatly illustrated in this observation of Thomas in his second week at school:

A large group of children (the majority) are making models of Daleks and painting them. Thomas does not like painting and tells the teacher he does not want to make one. He and another boy are given the choice of construction sets, plasticine or the home corner. They choose Octagon, a kit of small linking pieces and set to work to construct a space station. Thomas talks continuously, has lots of ideas and is very enthusiastic. The teacher comments that at the moment she is not pressurizing the newcomers but later in the term she will expect every child to take part in the planned activity.

Our new entrants did more imaginative and musical expression than older infants. They also spent more time watching and waiting, a natural consequence of uncertainty in a strange situation.

These observations indicate that transition might be eased if the gap between pre-school and infant activities was lessened by:

- the ability of adults in pre-schools to recognize a child's readiness for more complex tasks.

- the introduction of older pre-schoolers to activities they will encounter at school.

- a flexibility in the infant school which allows new entrants the
opportunity to continue some of their pre-school activities.

A question of choice

We have seen how the balance of activities changes as children make their
transition into school. But the biggest discriminator between pre-school
and infant school activities is the degree of choice children are given in
what they do.

Throughout our observations we noted the mode of choice which
prevailed: whether the children had free choice of all the activities available, choice from a limited range of options only, or no choice at all. One
mode might prevail for the whole group or there might be a combination
of different modes in operation at the same time, for instance free choice
for some children and no choice for others. Our findings are presented in
Table 2.

Table 2: Choice: Percentage of time for which various modes of choice prevailed
in 181 schools and pre-schools.

type of provision	none	limited	free	none & free	none & limited	limited & free	none, limited & free	%
Infant Class	67.0	4.9	12.1	3.8	11.2	0.8	0.2	100
Nursery Class	32.8	1.9	43.2	18.2	—	3.9	—	100
Nursery Unit	16.9	2.1	64.4	16.6	—	—	—	100
Nursery School	19.0	3.2	51.0	26.0	—	0.8	—	100
Playgroup	31.6	2.0	52.4	9.2	2.1	2.6	0.1	100
Day Nursery	41.3	6.8	42.8	3.5	2.4	1.2	2.0	100
Child- minder	17.3	18.7	62.9	0.3	0.6	0.2	—	100

The table shows clearly the prevalence of free choice in the pre-schools
and no choice in infant classes. In fact, our average infant class spent over
80 per cent of their time in limited or no-choice situations. We see here
the influence of the daily programme. There is no choice when the class

is required to come together for a specific purpose such as listening to a story, discussing news or moving to a radio music programme. Everyone engages in the same activity at the same time. Work tasks may be similarly organized: 'Write about the story of the Giant Turnip and draw a picture of it.' On the other hand children may be designated different tasks: 'Red group write your news, Blues do a number card and Greens paint a clown.' Either way there is no choice: activities are prescribed. When she has finished the child may be given a limited choice: 'Now you can play with the sand or do a puzzle', or a free hand: 'Now you can choose something.'

The latter prevails in pre-school provisions; the young child can choose freely from the activities which have been put out. There may be absolutely no restriction on her choice, or she may be expected to take part in at least one task. Here is a typical example of the degree of choice in a nursery unit. Naomi arrives to find the following activities set out in the playroom:

magnetic fishing; shape cards and mosaics; Fuzzyfelts; bucket scales with coloured bricks; brush-painting; jigsaw dice game; floor bricks and interlocking stepping stones; Wendy house, shop, dolls' house; books; dry sand; magnetic shapes; and a game called Rainbow Street.

After sampling two of these options, Naomi is called by the teacher to a group making bath salts for Christmas presents. Afterwards she can choose another activity.

We found that restrictions on choice in the pre-schools varied. No-choice situations were more prevalent in day nurseries where they were associated with domestic routines such as getting ready for meals and in private playgroups who tended to favour more adult-led formal group times. But lack of choice does not imply lack of enjoyment. No-choice situations in pre-schools largely consist of gatherings for stories and rhymes or drinks and biscuits. Here is an example of 'ring time' in Tamsin's playgroup:

It is eleven o'clock. The children carry their chairs to make a ring in the middle of the room. When they are ready one of the helpers comes round with mugs of orange squash. Tamsin follows her with the biscuit tin. Each child takes a biscuit and is encouraged to say thank you. When everyone has finished the beakers are collected to be washed. The leader starts singing and the children join in: 'Miss Polly had a dolly. . . .' Tamsin knows all the rhymes and does the actions. After the rhymes there is a count of all the children in the ring. They are asked 'Are there more boys than girls today?' and Tamsin shouts gleefully: 'No, we've won!'

For our target children transferring to school, choice represented a major discontinuity in their experience (Table B, Appendix). The children at home with mother or minder enjoyed most freedom. Those who went to nurseries and playgroups had free choice of activities for more than half the time. This was rather less for the children in nursery units because more time was taken up with school-oriented activities like registration and rehearsals for the Christmas concert. When they came to school, free choice time dwindled to less than a quarter, even with concessions made towards new entrants, and this was likely to become less as they got older.

Children react to this change in different ways. Here is a child who welcomed the stimulus of clearly defined tasks:

Nadia
attended a day nursery where the familiar activities no longer interested her and she stood around a great deal chatting to anyone who would listen. At school her class are gathered on the rug for word practice. The teacher holds up flashcards and the children call out the words. Nadia sits in rapt concentration oblivious of her companions, her eyes on the teacher. Next she is told to do a tracing. She sets to work eagerly and soon becomes totally absorbed, speaking to no one.

Next, a child for whom the lack of choice is stultifying:

Tracy
has transferred from a lively playgroup to a mixed-age infant class. While the older ones are doing their work, the five new entrants have been detailed to specific activities: sand, shop and floor bricks. Tracey plays alone at the shop. She sorts out the coins and talks to herself as she rings up prices on the cash register. After a few minutes she appears to have had enough. She looks around but there is nothing else on offer. She seems to think she has to stay where she is until told otherwise. She sits doing nothing.

Lastly, a child who does not like to be inactive and has found a way of maximizing her preferences:

Ruth

has moved from a large well-stocked unit into a reception class. She welcomes the opportunity to choose an activity when her work is done and makes eagerly for the sand tray. Soon the teacher says 'Tidy up time everybody, come and sit on the rug ready for story'. Ruth stays where she is. From time to time she peeps surreptitiously out from behind the screen which hides the sand tray. She realizes it will be some time before all the class are assembled and she makes the most of her chance to play. Eventually she joins the group on the rug. She is the last and has managed to prolong her sand play by four minutes.

Concluding remarks

In this chapter we have seen that what a child does at school and pre-school depends to a considerable extent on:

- availability of materials. What there is for him to do is influenced by the aims of the adults and the perceived function of their provision; money and the willingness to spend it; space for using and storing equipment; and a comprehensive knowledge of children's needs.

- accessibility of activities. Whether the child has access to an activity depends on organizational constraints imposed by the daily programme, time and large numbers; and the degree of choice he is given.

- personal preferences, inclinations and abilities.

We have noted four important changes as the child moves into infant school:

- the gradual shift in types of materials;

- the considerable swing in the balance of the curriculum;

- the explicit distinction between work and play, and the marked difference in freedom of choice.

So far we have discussed the child only in relation to his activities. We now turn to a consideration of the child in relation to the other children and adults present.

CHAPTER 6

Children and Adults

To understand how children spend their time it is not enough to know what they do. We also need to know a good deal about the dynamics of the situations in which their activities are carried out: the *modi operandi*. By far the most popular mode of operation in pre-schools is for children to have unlimited choice of the available activities while adults supervise or become involved from time to time. In infant classes the most prevalent mode is for children to be engaged in prescribed activities while the teacher is either actively involved with the class as a whole, or is taking the opportunity to hear individuals read or discuss their work while the rest are busy.

We can say that by these modes schools and pre-schools are clearly distinguished. But there are many factors operating here which interweave like the strands of a rope. To understand what such situations mean to a child we must unravel these strands and examine them singly as well as together. One way of doing this is to view the child in relation to the other children and adults present. Throughout our observations of activities we monitored not only the degree of choice children had but also how they were grouped and the extent to which adults were involved with them. This enables us to gain insights into children's experience by examining how much they work and play alone or together, and how much attention they receive and for what purpose.

The child and other children

Numbers great and small

The child coming into infant school is joining a society of which he is but one small member. That society is his class. At the same time he becomes also a member of a much larger society, the school. Schools and classes vary in size: classes in our sample ranged from ten to 34 and schools from 77 to 381. During the early weeks the new entrant is initiated and integrated into these societies. He learns which behaviours bring censure or approval; that he may not run and shout uninhibitedly but must conform to rules both explicit and implicit. On certain occasions he moves out of the security of his own classroom into the wider society beyond, joining some or all of the school for assembly and dinner, mingling with them on arrival, departure and at playtime. These occasions are dealt with in detail in Chapters 8, 9 and 10.

The noise and mass associated with large numbers may be a new and bewildering experience for young schoolchildren. Those whose only pre-school experience has been at home or with a minder will have been accustomed to playing alone or with no more than two or three other children; some of the smaller, private day nurseries cater for as few as five or six children. For all these youngsters the transition to school presents them with a sudden marked change in the size of the group to which they belong. Ian, who had attended playgroup for only one morning a week and spent the rest of the time at home with his mother, was frequently seen with his hands clapped firmly over his ears during the early weeks at school and would occasionally take himself off into a quiet corner to be alone for a few minutes. The majority of children, however, have had regular contact with large groups by the time they come to school. The sizes of the groups of children we observed in the various provisions is given below. Note the maximum of just over 30 in every type of provision:

day nurseries	5 to 31 children
playgroups	9 to 32 children
nursery schools, classes and units	13 to 34 children
infant classes	10 to 34 children

Some children, of course, find themselves transferring from a larger preschool into a smaller infant class. For example, thirty children attended Thomas' nursery school whereas there were only 18 in his reception class. But observations of our target children showed that the numbers of children they are with can fluctuate a good deal. At Thomas' nursery school the children went to their own groups for stories and discussions at the beginning and end of every session. Each group consisted of no more than ten children and had its own home base in a secluded area off the main playroom. Some nursery units operate in a similar way. In many day nurseries the children are allocated to rooms, each room serving as a base. The children mix freely for much of the day but return to their own room for stories, meals and rest.

With the exception of the children with minder or mother at home, considerable time was spent in crowds of 16 or more. Children in nursery education and playgroups can expect to spend most of their time in the presence of the whole unit, occasionally withdrawing physically into smaller, more intimate groups. For infants, on the other hand, this figure represents the basic unit of their class from which they move outwards into the society of the school beyond the classroom (see Appendix, Table C).

Tracey used to attend a playgroup for 26 children; now she goes to a combined first and middle school. Here is an example of the various crowds she encountered on a typical Monday morning in her first term:

assembly (whole school)	360
classroom activities	31
playtime (infants only)	170
special pre-reading group	9
television with another class	60
dinner (first sitting)	110

How did Tracey cope with these huge fluctuations? Her playgroup leader and her parents had described her as a 'withdrawn' child who preferred to play either alone, with her sister or with one special friend. In class she was quietly compliant and exhibited no sign of disturbance when she went with her class to the hall or another room. In pre-reading activities with a small group from her class she came to life and participated well. In the playground and at dinner she shied away from the noise and movement, seeking the refuge of her older sister and dissolving into tears if she could not find her. For this child the class represented stability in an otherwise shifting population. When the class dispersed she was alone in a whirling kaleidoscope of mass and confusion.

The class, then, is the infant's basic unit. But this unit is not static: within it children are constantly grouping and re-grouping, dispersing and reassembling.

Grouping

There are two kinds of grouping: that which is explicit and initiated by the adult in charge; and that which is spontaneous and initiated by the children. Because infant classes usually contain 20 or 30 pupils and only one adult, it is a common practice for teachers to organize their classes into groups. These may be temporary or permanent, clearly defined or flexible. In half our sample classes children were grouped according to ability, either remaining in these groups all the time or only for certain activities, particularly language and number tasks. In the rest of the sample, children were either grouped according to other criteria or not grouped at all. Other criteria included age, sex, behaviour and friendship. A few teachers organized their classes on a purely nominal basis into groups named after colours or animals: 'Lions can do painting today while Tigers and Monkeys finish their work cards.' Explicit grouping is organizational in intent. But during free choice situations children may form groups of a loose and unstructured nature to partake in the same activity.

There are three ways in which a class may function: as a whole unit, in groups, or as individuals. Children function as a whole unit when they operate as one group, either collectively as when listening to a story and writing news, or disparately as when choosing and intermingling, clearing up and playing in the playground. They function as groups when they are working on concurrent activities like number work, writing and painting. And they function as individuals when they are occupied separately on their own tasks. There are combinations of these modes: some children may be grouped while others work or play individually; the majority may be getting on with tasks while a single child receives attention from the teacher.

Throughout our observations we monitored the mode of grouping in operation and these are shown in Table 3. (The figures are derived from the cross-sectional study: see Chapter 3.)

Table 3: Grouping: Percentage of time for which various modes of grouping prevailed in 181 schools and pre-schools.

type of provision	as individuals	in groups	as a whole unit	groups and ungrouped	one child single from the rest	one child only	%
Infant classes	1.1	12.5	55.4	13.3	17.7	–	100
Nursery class	1.0	1.8	59.9	35.0	2.3	–	100
Nursery unit	2.7	1.7	55.5	37.8	2.3	–	100
Nursery school	2.2	10.6	39.7	47.5	–	–	100
Playgroup	1.3	4.5	54.8	36.6	2.8	–	100
Day nursery	1.6	6.8	73.2	13.8	4.6	–	100
Child-minder	3.2	–	71.8	–	1.4	23.6	100

The figures indicate that in schools and pre-schools the unit functioned as a whole for well over half the time. The second most popular mode was a mixture of grouped and ungrouped children. This is particularly favoured by nursery education and playgroups where it typifies free activity time: children go to activities of their own choice, playing independently or gathering around tables and in playcorners.

Children are found singly in some minders' homes, though in the majority of our sample there was more than one child. Singling children out from the rest is a feature peculiar to infant classes, occurring for nearly a fifth of the time in our sample. The teacher contrives to organize the class so that she can give personal tuition to one child at a time, hearing him read, helping with difficulties or showing him what to do next. This is a teaching style rarely found in pre-school provisions.

So far we have taken a holistic view and discussed the grouping patterns of children *en masse*. Now we turn to the social patterns of individuals in relation to other children.

Patterns of social behaviour

During observations of 36 target children transferring to school we noted whether their behaviour in relation to other children was solitary, parallel or interactive. These were defined as follows:

solitary: the child works or plays alone, or independently with material which is different from that used by children within speaking distance. His interest is centred upon his own activity and he pursues it without reference to what others are doing.

parallel: the child works or plays near another child or children using some or all of the same material as the others. He does not interact or try to influence the activity of the children near him.

interactive: the child is involved in activity with another child or children. They interact either verbally or non-verbally.

Social behaviour is idiosyncratic insofar as it depends on the child's temperament and his feelings towards his companions. However, there were some noticeable trends in the different types of provision and these are shown in Table 4. (These figures were derived from the longitudinal study: see Chapter 3.)

Table 4: Social behaviour: Percentage of time spent by 36 target children in different types of social behaviour. (N/A refers to time spent oriented solely towards an adult in a one-to-one situation.)

type of provision	solitary	parallel	interactive	N/A	%
Infant class	10.7	50.4	36.8	2.1	100
Nursery unit	11.8	46.5	40.2	1.5	100
Nursery school	21.0	29.6	46.3	3.1	100
Playgroup	10.6	34.2	50.8	4.4	100
Day nursery	17.1	27.7	52.9	2.3	100
Childminder	10.8	0.7	68.5	20.0	100
Own home	37.5	20.8	14.2	27.5	100

We found that the target children spent more time interacting with other children in their pre-schools than in their infant classes. Here is an example of interactive behaviour observed in a nursery school:

Thomas and his friend Jason are busy at one end of the playroom building a large construction out of bricks, boxes and a steering wheel. Thomas, who is directing the operation, gets very excited imparting ideas and instructions to Jason in a shrill voice. They argue as to whether it is finished or not and check over their handiwork closing all the gaps. Then they climb aboard and steam away towards a distant island.

Solitary behaviour was indulged in most by the child at home because for much of the time there were no other children to play with. For the children in pre-schools solo behaviour occurred usually in short bursts when they were bored, looking on at others, waiting for a friend or filling in time between more intensive activities. But several children spent longer periods alone particularly on occasions when their special friend was not there. Here is another observation of Thomas, this time when Jason was absent. Notice his lack of enthusiasm:

Thomas is at a loose end. He wants to do woodwork but there is not enough wood left. The teacher persuades him to paint the model he made yesterday. When he has finished, he places it in a sunny spot in the garden and settles down to watch it dry. The teacher strikes up a tune on the piano and children drift indoors for music time. Thomas does not move. He is invited to join in but shakes his head. Eventually he gets up and moves desultorily around the garden. He lets himself slowly down the slide several times; balances along the edge of the pond fitting his feet into each stone; dabbles half-heartedly with the sand-wheel. From time to time he pauses to see if his model is dry and resists all attempts to involve him in indoor activities.

At times a child's behaviour is not related to other children at all but is oriented solely to an adult in a one-to-one relationship. One-to-one situations occupied no more than a very small proportion of the time the child spent at school or pre-school. The picture was very different though for the children at home who spent a fifth or more of their time interacting with minder or mother (see also p. 86).

It was the children transferring from nursery units who exhibited least change in their social patterns on entering school. But for all the children starting school the biggest change was the increased amount of time spent in parallel behaviour. This accords with the higher incidence of compulsory group and whole unit activities in which the child participates alongside his peers but is passive towards them, such as watching a television programme, listening to the teacher giving instructions or explanations, and getting on with written work.

Children's grouping patterns and social behaviour cannot be divorced from the adults who are present in the provisions and it is to them we turn next.

The child and adults

Adult–child ratios

The ratio of adults to children has long been considered important, the assumption being that the younger the children are the more adults there should be available. From time to time recommendations have been put forward and targets set for more staff to fewer children. In 1973 the Department of Education and Science stated (in DES *Circular 2/73*) that staff ratios in nursery education of 1:13 would be 'generally acceptable'. The Ministry of Health (in *Circular 37/68*) recommended a minimum of 1:8 for playgroups. And although some local authorities may be more specific than others, their aim for day nurseries is usually 1:5, less if there are children under two, and not more than three children per minder.

During the cross-sectional study we were able to note the numbers of adults and children present for each session in all types of provision. We found that all the pre-school provisions had a considerably higher proportion of adults than the schools. While infant classes had only one adult for between 10 and 34 children, our sample pre-schools had one to seven or less. The nursery schools, classes and units were better staffed than those visited in the exploratory study, averaging ratios of 1:6 or 7. Play-groups averaged 1:5, day nurseries 1:4 or 5 and childminders 1:2 or 3.

But ratios like these must be interpreted carefully. The number of adults can fluctuate during a session as can the number of children present; and some of the adults may from time to time be busy in the kitchen or stacking toys away in the store place. A more accurate picture can be obtained by looking at individual experiences. In our study of target children we were able to monitor the ratio of adults present for every ten-minute period of observation. The results are shown in Table 5.

Table 5: Adult-child ratios: Percentage of time for which different adult-child ratios prevailed for 36 target children.

type of provision	1 to less than 10	1 to 10–15	1 to 16–20	1 to more than 20	%
Infant class	25	19	20	36	100
Nursery unit	43	31	8	18	100
Nursery school	90	10	–	–	100
Playgroup	94	3	2	1	100
Day nursery	73	19	6	2	100
Childminder	100	–	–	–	100
Private home	100	–	–	–	100

For children transferring to school, the change is of course greatest for those who have come straight from home or from a minder since they have been used to sharing their adult with no more than one or two others. We found that children from nursery school, playgroups and day nurseries suffered a serious discontinuity, being used to spending most of their time with about six children to an adult. Marked to a lesser extent was the change for children from nursery units who had sampled some of the more school-like large-group activities such as adult-led music and move-ment, radio programmes and concert rehearsals.

When they moved on to infant school most new entrants experienced for the first time the larger mass occasions like assembly and playtime when relatively few adults are present. On the other hand, they spent a quarter of the time in ratios of 1:8 or 9. There are two reasons for this. Firstly, new entrants are more likely to be withdrawn from their classes for pre-reading exercises or, in areas with large ethnic populations, for extra practice in English. Secondly, infant classes, particularly those with the youngest children, sometimes make use of auxiliary help in the form of a 'floating' teacher, the school's welfare assistant or parents who come in for short periods to lend a hand with certain activities.

The numbers of adults most often present when the target children were observed were: infant classes one, nursery units two, nursery school four, playgroups three or four, day nurseries two, childminders one. But these numbers rise and fall as various people come and go. Who are these people and what is their role?

Adult roles

Children at home spend most of their time in the company of their mother or minder but sometimes friends and relatives drop by and after school the older siblings come in. From time to time the social services adviser calls on the minder and occasionally a student nurse may come to observe.

Local authority day nurseries are staffed by trained nursery nurses and headed by an officer-in-charge. In addition there is likely to be a student nursery nurse gaining practical experience as part of her training. Some local authorities have arranged for qualified teachers to visit the nurseries on a part-time basis to take group activities, particularly with children who are approaching school age. The staff of private day nurseries may or may not be qualified though many of them are trained nursery nurses.

Playgroups are led by a supervisor, or sometimes a pair of supervisors who share responsibility, and may have up to five regular helpers. In addition, there may be one or two parents of playgroup children who come on a rota basis or stand in when a regular helper is absent. Some regular helpers are already qualified teachers or nurses and many of them (in 40 per cent of our sample playgroups) have taken a playgroup course.

Nursery education provisions are staffed by trained teachers and nursery nurses who often work in pairs. There may also be students in training from time to time and sometimes local secondary school pupils who visit weekly. Parent helpers were not much in evidence in our sample though this may vary from school to school. One nursery encouraged pensioners to come in one morning a week; they behaved like kindly grandparents and clearly enjoyed it as much as the children.

On transferring to infant school the child must become accustomed to spending two-thirds of his time with only one adult, the class teacher. From time to time he encounters other teachers and the head. If the school is fortunate enough to have a spare or part-time teacher, she might come in for brief periods to assist the class teacher. We found a small number of classes had students and occasionally secondary school pupils. In a few schools the welfare or general assistant lent a hand with messy activities or prepared materials. Comparatively few parent helpers were seen: they came on a regular basis to help with specific activities like cooking and sewing or manning the school library.

While it may be desirable to have a higher ratio of adults with younger children, it cannot be assumed that the more there are the better it will be for the child. A report on parent involvement in playgroups (PPA, 1980) points out that although the playgroup movement wants to draw in the parents, there is a danger of instability for the children if there are too many changes in adults during a play session. A study of staff in nursery education (Clift *et al.*, 1980) found that the quality of work in the nursery was critically affected by the number and type of adults present. The permanent staff achieved an optimum of involvement with the children when there were not more than three other helpers there. It is not enough, then, to attain high adult–child ratios. It is more important to consider what the adults are doing and how their presence affects the children.

Adult involvement

The extent to which the adults present were involved with the children was monitored continuously throughout our observations. In the cross-sectional study we scanned the area of observation at five-minute intervals noting not only what the children were doing but whether an adult was present at any of their activities. We found that in the pre-schools adults join all or most of the children for stories, rhymes and music. In play-groups they also sit with them at drink-and-biscuit time and in day nurseries for meals as well. At school the whole class joins with the teacher, not only for stories and music, but also for physical education and assembly, and adults are always present at playtime and at dinner. In both schools and pre-schools children tend to get on with all other types of activity whether an adult is present at the activity or not.

Presence at an activity does not necessarily mean that the adult is involved in it. But even a passive bystander may have an effect on the child. The Oxford Preschool Research Group (Bruner, 1980) reported that the mere presence of an adult was enough to double the length of time a child stayed at an activity.

The amount of time any one child spends in the company of an adult depends partly on the number of adults available and partly on personal preferences; a clinging child will seek out an adult more often than an independent one. When we observed target children individually we found that the minded child spent more than half his time near the adult. In nursery education and playgroups, children and adults spent a third of their time together at the same activity. Despite high ratios, the day nursery children spent only a fifth of their time in activities with an adult, no more than children in their early weeks at school.

It is not enough to know that adults were present at children's activities: we need to know what they were doing there. To this end we distinguished three levels of adult behaviour as follows: *involved:* the adult is actively involved in the children's activity; *patrolling:* the adult supervises the children and becomes involved with their activities briefly and intermittently; *supervising:* the adult supervises the children and is uninvolved in their activities.

Each of these levels or modes may operate for all the children at once or in combination. For example, if the teacher is telling a story to the whole class she is actively involved with all of them; if the class divides into groups, each group with an adult for story time, then involvement still prevails for everyone. But if the teacher listens to a child read while the rest get on with their work, then two modes are operating simultaneously, involvement for one child and tacit supervision for the rest.

We continuously recorded the modes of adult involvement which were in operation in each provision and the results are presented in Table 6.

Table 6: Adult involvement: Percentage of time for which various modes of adult involvement prevailed in 181 schools and pre-schools.

type of provision	involved with one or some	involved with all	patrolling all	patrolling & supervising	supervising all	%
Infant classes	29.1	26.3	14.0	2.5	28.1	100
Nursery class	27.5	18.6	17.9	4.3	31.7	100
Nursery unit	33.8	27.6	17.5	3.3	17.8	100
Nursery school	43.3	19.7	17.6	3.9	15.5	100
Playgroup	36.5	20.4	10.4	3.7	29.0	100
Day nursery	16.0	21.7	6.9	1.3	54.1	100
Child-minder	3.0	14.5	15.7	–	66.8	100

The greatest discriminator between provisions is the mode of supervision for all. This is the lowest level of involvement: in fact when this mode prevails the adults are not actively involved with any child. This mode occurred most for minded and day nursery children where it prevailed for well over half the time. Minders are busy with household chores, and the children, though not far away, get on with amusing themselves. In day nurseries, particularly the local authority ones, this high incidence of non-involvement is surprising in view of their high adult–child ratios. Non-involvement was lowest in the nursery schools where staff were actively involved with at least some of the children for all but 15 per cent of the time.

Involvement of any kind, whether with individuals, groups or the whole, was highest in nursery schools and units. But styles varied between provisions. Nursery school staff favoured a combination of patrolling and involvement, some remaining at one activity while others went about lending a hand where needed. In nursery units, on the other hand, there were more adult-led activities, either with all the children or with small groups while the rest played freely. This latter style, where adults sit down and direct specific activities with small groups of children, was popular in the playgroups; for example, while groups were being shown how to make bead necklaces or pastry shapes, other helpers might be preparing drinks in the kitchen or clearing away toys. Infant teachers were involved in some way for more than 70 per cent of the time. Mostly this was either formally with the class as a whole or with one child at a time; to a lesser extent they also went around the class checking work and giving tuition.

It appears, then, that adults have different styles of working with children and these vary considerably between different types of provision. How does this affect the child who is transferring to school? How much attention is he likely to get?

Adult attention

Although adults may be very busy talking to children and involving themselves in their activities, any one child may in fact receive very little attention personally. Because we observed target children individually we were able to monitor the attention each one received. We distinguished three kinds of attention:

that which is given to the child as an individual; that which is given to a group of which the child is a member; and that which is given to the whole unit of which the child is a member.

The results are shown in Table 7.

Table 7: Adult attention: Percentage of time for which 36 target children received attention.

type of provision	as an individual	as one of a group	as one of whole unit	total attention	no attention	%
Infant class	2.3	3.7	26.2	32.2	67.8	100
Nursery unit	1.7	14.4	25.7	41.8	58.2	100
Nursery school	3.1	23.8	4.6	31.5	68.5	100
Playgroup	5.2	9.7	19.3	34.3	65.7	100
Day nursery	2.7	5.5	9.0	17.2	82.8	100
Childminder	36.9	0.8	18.5	56.2	43.8	100
Private home	28.3	0.8	–	29.1	70.9	100

The day nursery children received considerably less attention than any of the others, a finding compatible with the generally low level of adult involvement in their activities. The minded child, whom we know spent more than half his time alongside the adult, received most attention. The children who transferred to school from nursery school, playgroups and home were given roughly the same total amount of attention before and after transition. But because there are fewer adults and more children at school the attention was of a different kind. The children at home with mother or minder were given mostly personal attention in a one-to-one relationship. In all the other pre-school provisions there was very little personal attention, children being dealt with in groups both large and small. When they moved into school each child had to become accustomed to being treated as part of a unit since most of the attention he received was when the teacher addressed the class as a whole.

It seems logical to suppose that the children who had been used to plenty of individual attention might have difficulty adjusting to whole class activities. In fact the minded boy had also attended a playgroup and was observed to be relaxed and confident at school; at story time, when he was one of 35 children, he 'sat very still and attentive throughout'. Celia, who had not been away from home before, was more subdued. On her first morning at school the class watched *Playschool*, a television programme she had watched regularly at home. Celia was attentive but did not join in the singing and when the rest of the class shouted their responses she looked on in silence.

The day nursery children who had received relatively little attention of any kind reacted in different ways. They appeared to find formal class activities like music, physical education and stories enjoyable and stimulating. But they sometimes failed to respond when the teacher was giving a direction to the whole class; perhaps they thought it did not apply to them personally. Of course, this kind of behaviour is not exclusive to children from day nurseries but one would expect it to occur more in children who have been unused to being spoken to in a mass. Here is an observation of Sundar on his third day at school:

At playtime the children line up to go outside. Despite repeated instructions to 'make a straight line' Sundar wanders off alone down the corridor and out to the playground.

We do not know how much this kind of behaviour is due to genuine difficulty or deliberate obtuseness. But occasions when children were obviously not complying with adults' wishes were comparatively rare, occupying less than two per cent of their time in any provision. The difficulty of subduing one's individuality to the common cause was neatly expressed by Nadia who, when told to put her finished work with the others on the teacher's desk, exclaimed indignantly 'But this is MY picture'.

Adult–child interaction

To discover for what purpose children receive attention we monitored the interactions which occurred between adults and our target children. An interaction was defined as any episode of behaviour involving the child and an adult or adults; it may be verbal or non-verbal. Every time an interaction occurred we noted who initiated it, how it was initiated, to whom it was directed, the nature of the response, the length of the interaction and its content or function. This enabled us to ask the following questions about adult–child interaction.

1. HOW MUCH ADULT/CHILD INTERACTION OCCURRED?
The children at home interacted more often with their minder or mother than children with adults in any other provision. Interactions were least frequent for the children in day nurseries; this accords with low levels of attention and involvement.

Children usually made contact with one adult at a time. Adults, on the other hand, spoke not only with individual children but also with groups of all sizes from pairs to the whole unit. For the minded and home children contacts were mostly of a one-to-one kind, but the other pre-schoolers were addressed personally only half the time. When they transferred to school there were even fewer opportunities for individual contact with the teacher and the new entrant had to become accustomed to being more often addressed with the whole class.

The table below shows the average number of contacts initiated per hour in the different provisions with target children, both in one-to-one situations and as a member of a group.

type of provision	one-to-one	in a group	total
infant classes	6	7	13
nursery units	8	8	16
nursery schools	9	5	14
playgroups	10	7	17
day nurseries	6	6	12
childminder	18	5	23
child at home	36	7	43

2. WHO INITIATED THE INTERACTIONS?

The children at home with minder or mother initiated more than half their interactions themselves. For the rest, more were begun by the adults, particularly those in nursery units. When they transferred to school, relationships became even more adult-directed with the teachers starting nearly three-quarters of all interactions.

3. HOW WERE INTERACTIONS INITIATED?

The majority of all interactions were begun verbally by children and adults. But adults sometimes attracted the attention of a class or group by clapping their hands before addressing them; in the school playground teachers might gather children together by ringing a bell or blowing a whistle. Occasionally individual children were approached non-verbally, the adult pausing to fasten a child's painting apron, wipe his nose or help him down the slide.

Most children attracted an adult's notice by speaking to her. Exceptionally, the playgroup children used non-verbal signals more than other pre-schoolers to get attention. Signals included physically approaching the adult, smiling at her, taking her hand, tugging her sleeve, crying and making noises. A similar amount of non-verbal contact was made by children at school but in a different manner: by raising a hand for attention or by taking work to the teacher for her inspection.

4. WHAT KIND OF RESPONSE DID THEY GET?

Responses to bids for attention were of three kinds:
- non-response: the initiation was either ignored or there was no observable response.
- a brief acknowledgement, either verbal or non-verbal.
- a response which developed into a two-way exchange or conversation.

Roughly one-sixth of all attempted contacts appeared to be ignored by adults and children alike, except by those at nursery school who were more responsive to each other. Perhaps adults have to screen out a certain amount of children's attention-seeking in order to cope, particularly if they are busy. Children failed to respond most often in whole-unit situations both at school and pre-school. Like Sundar, young children often do not realize that mass instruction includes them personally. The majority of all contacts were greeted with a brief acknowledgement or short reply which concluded the interaction.

Two-way exchanges or conversations developed most often between the children at home and their minder or mother. For the other pre-schoolers, less than a quarter of all contacts led to a conversation. Even fewer conversations took place between teacher and child at infant school. There was a better chance of dialogue developing if contact was initiated by the child, though it was usually the adult who did most of the talking.

5. WHAT WERE INTERACTIONS ABOUT?

The content or function of interactions can be grouped into three types:

managerial: to do with management and organization, e.g. 'Sit on a chair everyone'; 'Put your apron on Christine'.

personal or social: to do with the person and his feelings, or with his family, e.g. 'What a pretty dress', 'Let me wipe your nose', 'I've got a new baby'.

substantive: to do with the substance of the activity the child is engaged in, e.g. 'Does it sink or float', 'You trace round it like this'.

When adults spoke to children the purpose was usually managerial; at least two-thirds of their remarks were of this type, even more in day nurseries and infant schools. The Oxford Preschool Research team, in a detailed study of verbal exchanges in playgroups and nursery schools (Wood *et al.*, 1980), reported a similar emphasis on management.

Interactions of a social or personal nature were rarely initiated by staff in infant and nursery education, occurring more often in playgroups and day nurseries with individual children. However, comments performing a substantive or 'teaching' function occurred most during formal group sessions at nursery school and in one-to-one tutorials at infant school. Indeed, the tendency for staff in different types of provision to favour either social or substantive talk is compatible with their expressed aims which gave more weight to care or education. Children's contacts with adults were more or less equally divided between managerial, substantive and personal matters except in the day nurseries where more social talk occurred.

6. HOW LONG DID INTERACTIONS LAST?
The majority of all interactions between adults and children were short, lasting less than 30 seconds. Only about 15 per cent of all contacts lasted longer. The most common contacts, then, between adults and children in schools and pre-schools are fleeting exchanges to do with management and organization.

Summing up

The child starting school is joining a society with larger numbers of children than he has hitherto encountered. The number of children with whom he has to share an adult will also be greater than ever before. Whether he has come straight from home or from a pre-school, these facts are crucial in bringing about changes in his experience. The management of large numbers of children by comparatively few adults imposes organizational constraints on both school and class. These have the following implications for the new entrants:

- a programme which entails the child moving out from his base group or class from time to time to join larger crowds of children who may be older, bigger and noisier than himself.

- mass events such as playtime, dinnertime and assembly at which the adults may be few or unfamiliar.

- the presence of only one adult for most of the time in class.

- the grouping of children within the class.

- an increase in parallel behaviour when the child must participate alongside his peers in whole-class or large-group activity.

- fewer opportunities for interactive play.

- the singling of individuals for brief bouts of personal tuition while the rest of the class are busy.

- few opportunities for conversation with an adult on a one-to-one basis.

- being spoken to en masse.

Children sooner or later adapt to these changes. There are those who appear to enjoy the stimulus of more structured activity and competition with their peers at group-time. We saw one or two children blossom with less adult intervention. But signs of distress associated with the presence of large numbers of children and small numbers of adults were observed:

- impatience at having to wait for the teacher's attention.

- covering the ears to shut out noise.

- bewilderment and dismay in mass situations.

- failure to respond to instructions given en masse.

- inability to keep still and quiet for sustained periods.

- unwillingness to pool creative work.

The following strategies were employed by some staff to ease the transition:

- pre-school training in sitting still, listening and not shouting out.

- pre-school practice in being spoken to as a group and responding to instructions.

- keeping the reception class together in the early weeks to give the child a chance to get to know his classmates and establish a relationship with his teacher.

- introducing gradually attendance at mass events like playtime, assembly and dinnertime with younger children at first being secluded from the rest.

- in mixed age-groups, seating new entrants near the teacher for easy access.

- allowing new entrants to jump the queue because they need more frequent attention from the\teacher.

- using auxiliary adult help especially for activities where children need a lot of assistance.

- strengthening teacher–child bonds by calling children by name and using eye-contact in group situations.

Given existing adult–child ratios, it requires great skill on the teacher's part to make each child feel a valued individual.

CHAPTER 7

The Part Parents Play

It is tempting to think of children only as attenders of pre-schools or pupils at infant schools. But they spend far less time in these situations than they do at home. So a study of children's experiences would be seriously lacking if it ignored that powerful mediator of continuity, the family, and in particular the part played by parents.

To examine the subtle ways in which the family can influence a child's transition to school, we would need to be a fly on the wall in his home over a long period and this was beyond the brief of this project. However, in an attempt to discover something of the part parents play in the transition process, we visited the home of each target child before and after he started school to talk with his parents in informal interviews lasting several hours. We sought their attitudes to school and pre-school, and their hopes and fears for their youngster's success. We also interviewed staff in schools and pre-schools about their attitudes to parents, their contacts with them and their expectations for the children.

Parents and pre-school

Before their children started school, many parents already had aspirations for their youngsters. Schooling was to be valued and they wanted their children to go as far as possible but without pressure. A few parents had specific jobs in mind, like teaching or accountancy, but the majority took the view that the child should be allowed to follow his own preferences while they gave him the required support.

On the brink of their educational careers, all but one of our 36 target children were attending some kind of pre-school provision. Yet one in five parents dismissed this as of no real value because 'it doesn't really teach them anything.' The rest clearly thought their children had learnt something and specified the social benefits of mixing, sharing and taking turns; and the cognitive gains of knowing letters, numbers, colours, shapes and nursery rhymes. They also felt that going to pre-school had given their youngsters a better start in life and introduced them to a measure of discipline and control. One or two mentioned incipient problems which had been spotted early and, for themselves, the therapeutic benefit of a willing ear. A small proportion of parents, particularly those of French, Indian and Chinese origins in our sample, felt that their children were wasting precious time which could be spent in more academic learning.

This notion of what constitutes 'learning' and 'wasting time' is in conflict with professional beliefs about the purpose of play activities for the under-fives. In fact, most of the parents saw a sharp distinction between the function of pre-school staff who 'just keep them amused', 'supervise their play', and 'organize the paint and biscuits'; and infant teachers who 'have to keep up standards', 'have a proper learning pro-gramme' and 'get cracking with teaching them'. These popular sentiments were neatly summed up by the father who said 'Of course one is a play school and the other is a learning school'.

Starting school, then, is clearly viewed as a step: a step from the stage of playing to the stage of proper learning. What gives rise to this view in the minds of parents? Is it born of acquaintance with the facts or coloured by memories of their own experience?

We found that among pre-school staff opinion was divided between those in nursery education who saw all learning as a continuous process, and those in day nurseries and playgroups who distinguished the social training and groundwork they provided from the teaching which would follow at school. Infant teachers, on the other hand, shared the parents' view that it was they who provided the trained expertise of their profession and began to 'teach'. Teaching was defined in terms of transmitting specific skills, like reading. Transferring to school was thus conceived by parents and infant teachers alike as making a new start, taking a big step forward, achieving status; it was an acknowledged disruption in the flow of children's experience.

Does this mean that staff in nursery education failed to communicate their conception of learning as a continuous process? Teresa Smith in her study of parents and pre-school (1980) concludes that far more could be done to explain pre-school aims and methods to parents. Furthermore, our own study suggests that what is required is a radical reversal from the popular view of education as 'being taught' to a view of education as a life-long process of learning.

What opportunities are there for pre-school staff to explain their aims and methods? Very few of our target parents made any reference to the array of talks and courses offered, for example, by the Pre-school Play-groups Association to parents, playgroup helpers and anyone interested in young children. We found that the majority of the parents' contacts with pre-schools consisted in bringing and fetching their children. But although the child was usually welcomed, there was often no exchange between staff and parents. In most pre-schools parents could accompany their children inside but their stay was usually very brief. In the nursery units and some of the playgroups an invisible boundary kept the parents at a distance and demarcated the place where they could wait to collect their children. Parent access tended to be more free and easy in day nurseries where children were brought and fetched at different times, but working mothers rarely had time to linger. In playgroups there was contact between parent and supervisor when fees were paid, but again mothers tended to hasten away to make the most of their brief spell of freedom. Verbal contact was usually initiated by the parent who had something specific to inform the staff about. One nursery unit allowed parents to come inside twenty minutes early one day a week for the purpose of discussing any problems they might have.

Some provisions created alternative opportunities for parent–staff contact. Since in nursery units arrival and departure times were not considered convenient, open evenings were held termly when parents were invited to inspect the nursery and talk with the staff. Some day nurseries, mindful of giving family support, arranged regular weekly meetings with talks and demonstrations, and social events such as sports, parties and outings. All types of provision, especially the playgroups, held fund-raising events like jumble sales and coffee mornings, but reported that it was always the same few parents who supported them. Some parents willingly mended toys and equipment or cared for the nursery's pets during weekends and holidays. But nowhere was there evidence of a deliberate attempt to explain a pre-school's aims and methods to parents during the period of this study.

The belief is widely held among educationists that cooperation between parents and pre-school is a good thing. Woodhead (1979) says that 'if cooperation with parents is achieved at both stages (pre-school and in-fant), then there is a sound foundation on which to build the continuous process of learning'. The aim of such cooperation (Hughes *et al.*, 1980) is 'to counterbalance the staff's skills and expertise with the parents' own views and knowledge, so that a more equal partnership between the two can develop'. We saw evidence of cooperation between parents and pre-school which had obvious benefits for the child. Here is one example:

Nick attended a nursery unit where he was at first described as sullen and withdrawn. After a turbulent period of rows and shouting his parents eventually separated. His mother was very upset and confided her problems to the nursery staff who interpreted Nick's behaviour in the light of his home life. The family had been living in a 'tied' house and when the father left they faced the threat of losing their home. The nursery teacher wrote to the local housing department in an attempt to help the family. Some months later, Nick and his mother settled into a new flat and after a period of relative stability Nick was reported to be 'a different child' and progressing well. Both mother and teacher attributed the change partly to the support and security the nursery was able to provide in response to being told about Nick's home circumstances.

Cooperation may be extended beyond the sharing of information to the sharing of experience. One of the expressed aims of the playgroup move-ment is to involve parents. Involvement, according to a recent report by the Pre-School Playgroups Association (PPA, 1980), 'begins with a feel-ing, leads on to action, and at every stage carries with it responsibility – responsibility in person relationships, responsibility for undertaking and carrying out tasks, and shared responsibility for decision-making'. But not all playgroup leaders want to involve parents. Reasons given by our sample included fear of children misbehaving if their mother was present and reluctance to make use of people who were paying for a service. On the other hand some supervisors felt that many mothers were unrespon-sive. Nearly half our target mothers said they had never had the chance to help at playgroup or nursery but would love to if asked. Only three were regular helpers and a few had stepped in on occasions when needed. If the rest were unwilling they were reluctant to admit it. Perhaps a greater readiness on both sides to exploit this potential source of parent interest would lead to a clearer understanding of the role of pre-school in the learning process.

Parents and transition

If parents see starting school as a big step, how will this attitude affect the child?

As entry day drew near, we asked our target parents whether they had ever talked to their children about going to school. Nearly a third of them confessed that they avoided the subject or referred to it as little as possible. They viewed the transfer with some trepidation and were deliberately playing it down so as not to put the child off. In families with older siblings, talk about school was a natural part of the everyday conversation. But parents who made a point of mentioning it did so with varying degrees of cheerful anticipation, reassurance or threat. Children were encouraged to look forward to learning to read and write, playing games, doing painting, wearing a uniform and meeting new friends. They were re-assured about noise and crowds, and comforted with the thought that their older brothers and sisters would be there and their mother would meet them at the end of the day. One or two exasperated parents used school as a dire warning to those who wet the bed or would not do up their own shoes: 'You'll have to grow up when you get to school'.

Two out of three parents thought their child would take to school quite well and did not foresee any problems. Many felt their children were ready for school; they were bored at home, fed up with nursery and the time was ripe to move on. Others were more cautious, anticipating either the shock of the first day or an increasing reluctance to attend when the novelty wore off.

Asked whether they had ever been to their child's new school the majority said they had, though with only a month to go there were still a few who were waiting for some word from the school. Many parents had accepted an invitation to visit the school with their child in the term before entry. Most schools held these pre-entry visits during the day so that prospective new entrants could see normal activities in progress. Additionally, a few schools held evening meetings for the parents only. Usually there was only one pre-entry visit, though in some schools there were opportunities for the children to come in regularly once a week. First visits tended to be variations on the following theme:

the child arrives with her parents at the appointed time along with other intending pupils. The head teacher speaks to all of them briefly. The children are taken on a tour of the school and then shown into a classroom or introduced to their new teacher. They are then provided with activities to do, while their parents are addressed and given a cup of tea.

Of course, some parents are already familiar with the school because they have older children there and have attended the highlights like concerts, sports day and open evenings as well as taking and fetching daily. All our parents had made a preliminary acquaintance with the school when they had enrolled their child as much as two years earlier. But only one in four had actually met the reception teacher by the time their child started school. The parents generally at this stage had warm and positive attitudes towards their child's new school. First impressions ranged from the abundance of pictures on the walls, the colour of the paint and the tropical fish tank to the friendly atmosphere.

Choice of school was limited, most parents sending their children to the one which served their area. Where there was more than one infant school parents gave positive reasons for their choice. A school was selected because it was:

convenient: closest to home or finishing at a time which fitted the family routine

familiar: older siblings or friends went there, the school had been visited or the teacher was known personally

pleasant: the staff were nice, the dinners good, the atmosphere happy

better than another school: it had a good reputation, more or less discipline and structure, or a more individual approach.

Newly-opened schools were regarded with a certain amount of suspicion and a 'better the devil we know' attitude.

Most parents felt that starting school would be considerably easier for the child if he could do certain things for himself. The most important was being able to cope with himself away from his mother: getting dressed, eating dinner, going to the toilet. The importance of personal independence was also stressed by pre-school staff, some of whom made a point of showing the children how to do up shoes or eat with a knife and fork. Infant teachers said it was most useful if new entrants could cope with their own buttons, buckles and zips, use the toilet, blow their noses and look after their own belongings. Everyone agreed that a five-year-old should know his own address, be able to speak up for himself and not be afraid to ask anything. Staff in schools and pre-schools thought the child should be able to share and mix with others; and infant teachers agreed with playgroup leaders that being able to sit still, listen, follow instructions and tidy up were all advantageous when starting school. Parents and teachers thought that certain cognitive skills, like knowing letters and simple numbers, give the child a better start; and others added that he should know colours, recognize his own name and be able to use a pencil, paintbrush and scissors. Reception teachers would like their new pupils to be used to handling books and being read to, but both parents and pre-school staff were wary of anything which might suggest they were teaching children to read: 'You shouldn't educate them to know words, that's the teacher's job'.

Everyone had plenty of hints to offer to parents of children starting school. Here is a selection of the most popular ones.

Parents to parents:

Take an interest in what your child says and follow it through at home.

Take your child to meet his teacher and regard her as a friend.

Give him plenty of time to get ready, don't rush him.

Take your child to school and be there to meet him.

Go with your child into the classroom.

Let him come home to dinner at first.

Pre-school staff to parents:

Encourage a positive attitude to school, whet his appetite and treat school as a privilege, not a threat.

Don't pressure him to achieve too much too soon.

Consult the teacher on how best to help him.

Infant head teachers to parents:

Accustom your child to being away from you.

Teach him to stand up for himself without being aggressive.

Talk to him, read to him and extend his vocabulary.

Bring your child past the school and let him watch the children playing in the playground.

If you have a son, teach him to use a urinal.

Parents also had ideas about how the infant school could make life easier for new entrants. They offered the following suggestions:

Let the children visit more often before they start; it can be two months between the pre-entry visit and the beginning of the next term, especially for September starters.

Explain everything to them so they don't feel scared.

Show them around and tell them where everything is.

Encourage them to ask when they don't know something.

Separate the new ones at playtime and have someone to look after them.

Let parents go into the classroom with their children.

Let the children wait indoors till they are collected.

Be lenient on their eating habits.

Parents on the whole thought their children would welcome the stimulus of school activities and would delight in 'proper' learning, particularly writing and reading. Accession to the infants school would bring its own kudos: the child would feel more grown-up like his older siblings or friends. On the other hand, many parents expressed anxieties. They worried that their child might not be able to cope with school dinners or the playground; he might not take kindly to the restricted freedom, to the discipline, to having to sit still at a desk or to the long day; he might feel small and get bullied by the bigger children. While they sought to reassure their offspring, the parents themselves needed reassurance.

Parents and infants school

A month or so after our target children started school we interviewed their parents again. We found that while a few had viewed the transition with equanimity, most mothers saw it as a milestone in their own lives. Emotions ranged from dismay: 'It'll be such a wrench when he's gone' to elation: 'I'll be able to start living again'. When the great day came mothers confessed to feelings of gladness, sadness and apprehension. They were glad for the child so long as he was happy and glad for themselves that they had more time. They were apprehensive about how he would settle and whether he would eat his dinner. They were sad when they realized he was not a baby any more, and missed his company around the house. As one mother said, 'It was the longest day of my life!'

A third of our target children were deemed by their parents to have settled in well from the beginning with no apparent problems. But the rest were described as not keen at first. Symptoms that all was not well were: crying at the start, on coming home or after a few days; wanting to go back to pre-school; being over-tired; being afraid of the crowds, the playground or the bigger children; having toilet accidents; complaining about the constraints on activities; being quiet and withdrawn. By the end of the first month things had improved; two out of three were described as enthusiastic and loving school. This was a rather more optimistic view than that observed by the researchers who were in the privileged position of being able to watch the children at school. While parents noticed things like persisting tiredness and heard their children's complaints, the observers were able to see difficulties as they occurred during the day and noted the prevalence of recurring problems especially with playtime and school meals (see Chapters 9 and 10).

The majority of the new entrants were reported to like and even adore their teacher, though a few mentioned her so rarely that their parents were prompted to ask the researcher how their child got on with his teacher. Half the parents described the teacher as particularly suited to their own child's needs because she was lively, firm, caring, sympathetic, warm, gentle or patient. The rest either did not know her well enough or felt a month was too short to tell.

Most of the children had at some time said they did not want to go to school. Some had given no reason; others had complained of feeling unwell, or expressed dislike of school in general or of PE and dinners in particular. Parents reacted in different ways. They comforted: 'Never mind, you'll be all right when you get there'; they coerced: 'Don't be silly, you have to go to school'; or they ignored, changed the subject and kept walking. Persistent refusal did not seem to be a problem.

Asked whether they had noticed any changes in their child since he had started school, almost all the parents said they had. Children were described as more grown-up, independent, sensible, obedient and affectionate; speech and appetites had improved. But children had also become more irritable, aggressive, bossy, rude and noisy; they picked up 'bad' language and developed tantrums. They competed more with older siblings, were less tolerant of younger ones. They amused themselves more at home by playing schools, reading, writing and drawing.

There had been changes too in family routines: the child went to bed earlier, got up earlier; meal times had been adjusted. Some working mothers had changed their job hours to fit in with the child's homecoming.

Parents were divided on whether to ask their child about his school life or whether to let him offer information spontaneously. While some children freely related the incidents and activities of their day, others answered the question 'What did you do today?' with 'Nothing' or 'I've forgotten.' Most of the children from time to time brought things home from school such as art and craft work, library or reading books and lists of words to learn. One in four had not been allowed to bring anything home and parents thought this a pity and took it as a sign that the school feared parental pressure. Most of the children wanted to practise at home things they had done at school: writing, drawing and colouring, songs and rhymes, and parents liked to encourage them. But attempts by teachers to capitalize on this willingness to help can misfire if there is insufficient understanding of the motive. One teacher, seeing a boy's difficulty, sent home a pair of scissors so that he could practise cutting out. His mother's reaction was one of affronted indignation: 'The only reason he can't cut out at school is because the stupid scissors are blunt!' Feelings about their child taking things to school from home were mixed. Opinion was divided between those who discouraged it because things get lost and broken, or the school would not approve; and those who encouraged their children to take things which they considered to be of an 'educational' nature, or which had been specifically requested by the teacher.

The child, then, is a potential channel of communication between home and school. He inhabits both and what he brings from one to the other in word or kind gives parent and teacher a brief glimpse of each other's worlds. But what about direct contact between parents and school?

Of the 36 sets of parents, only two had had no contact with the staff of their child's new school since he had started. The majority of contacts were between mother and class teacher. They usually consisted of brief and casual encounters when taking and fetching the children each day. For the first few days at least, the children were accompanied by a parent, working mothers usually making special arrangements to be with their children. Later on, a few children were escorted by older siblings, friends or minders, but the majority continued to be escorted by their mother throughout the early weeks. Procedures at arrival and departure time varied from school to school and usually evolved as the term advanced. At the beginning parents could usually accompany their children into the school, even into the classroom. But sooner or later the place of parting retreated further from the classroom, as did the spot for meeting again at the end of the day. It was as if a boundary became established beyond which parents waited for their children. The waiting place could be the entrance hall, the playground outside the classroom, the fringes of the playground, the end of the drive or even outside the school grounds. Why the waiting place became established where it did was not always clear. In some cases it was made explicit by the school: parents were told that after the first week they should not come into the building but wait outside in the playground. Practical reasons were important: parents added to the congestion of crowded corridors, they were a distraction outside classroom windows, they could be a hazard to traffic. Boundaries which were not made explicit may have been dictated by the layout of the premises and by the parents' own wish not to intrude. In open-plan schools it was easier for mothers to wait close to the entrance of their child's classroom while still remaining outside the building; in corridor schools they were more remote. But where mothers were allowed free access to the class-room, their visit was usually fleeting and they withdrew as rapidly as possible.

Boundaries in the infant schools were more rigid and remote than any observed in the pre-schools. Yet very few parents agreed that they would wish to linger in the classroom. The consensus of opinion was that, even if it were permissible for the mother to stay in the early days, it would only delay the parting and make it harder for the child. The best plan was to see the child settled and then leave.

As boundaries recede further from the classroom, opportunities for spontaneous contact between parent and teacher decrease and a deliberate approach must be made if one wishes to speak to the other. Approaches of this kind were more often made by parents than teachers. Some mothers had reason to speak to the teacher or head about specific matters such as the child's reluctance to come to school, his worries about dinner, his ailments or his progress. Occasionally notes were sent, but more often contact of this nature was personal. Head teachers tended to be approached less often than class teachers, several mothers expressing awe of them.

The concept of approachability is subtle and complex. There was a noticeable mismatch in our study between the way staff saw themselves and their approachability in the eyes of the parents. Most staff expressed an openness towards parents: 'They can come and see us any time they want'. But many parents did not feel they could. There was a minority who had an easy relationship with the school and found the staff welcoming and friendly: 'They are very approachable, they give you the impression that yours is the only child they're teaching'. But for most parents, access was complicated by feelings about the staff's professionalism, their own self-image and memories of their own schooldays. Some heads specified that parents should make an appointment or come in after school; others said 'Just walk in anytime'. Parents' reactions were mixed, ranging from the considerate: 'I would go if necessary but not when they're busy' and the cautious: 'I don't want to seem over-protective and fussy' to the ebullient: 'I wouldn't be afraid to go; if I wasn't satisfied I'd take him away anyway'.

Clearly there exists a 'them and us' attitude in varying degrees. Some heads tried to bridge the gap by displaying invitations to walk in or noticeboards for exchange and mart. Others made direct offers of opportunities for contact in the early weeks including coffee mornings, a weekly surgery when the teacher was available after school, and invitations to assembly. These offers were not always taken up, particularly by parents who had younger children or who went out to work. But relationships are personal, and rapport between staff and parents depends so much on the ability of the people concerned to establish it. The cheerful confidence expressed by some parents was offset by the majority who seemed to regard the staff with uncertainty tinged with distrust, and a sensitivity so prickly that a contact could be destroyed at a word: 'A teacher said 'Yes?' and I immediately felt I shouldn't have been there'.

Perhaps relationships will improve and strengthen with time. There would certainly be opportunities for further contact with schools who were planning 'open' days or evenings and fund-raising events. Some heads welcomed parents' help in making paths and sandpits or putting up shelves; others invited mothers to help with specific activities like cooking and sewing, to help children get dressed after swimming or run the school library; or to do classroom chores like sharpening pencils, covering books and washing paintpots. A note of caution was sounded by those who said, 'You have to pick your parents' and 'You have to draw a line so they don't take over'. Disappointment was expressed at the poor response in areas where there was a high proportion of immigrant families or working mothers. Philosophies ranged from those who believed in protecting the professionalism of the teacher to those who saw themselves as educators of parents as well as children. The first is compatible with an attitude which keeps parents at arm's length, the second with the view that the more contact there is the better: 'Even if they only come in for coffee they feel they have a stake in their kid's education, they don't feel they're on the outside'.

But do parents want a stake in their children's schooling? One thing was clear from our study – they at least wanted more information about their children's schooling. They envied the researcher's role of 'fly on the classroom wall' and wanted to see how their child spent his day. They specifically wanted to know how the teacher coped with a wide age range, how letters were taught, what modern maths was like and what happened on wet days. One head responded to this curiosity by inviting parents to 'come and see for yourselves', believing that the more they saw of the school the wiser they would become to its methods and rationale. The desire for something more than peripheral contact was echoed by the parent who said, 'We need to understand what they do, not just help at the fair'.

Understanding, then, could be the key to developing more positive attitudes and overcoming apathy, nervousness and suspicion. In 1967 the Plowden Report said, 'There will have to be constant communication between parents and the schools if the aims of the schools are to be fully understood'. Our sample schools had made a start in the right direction. All of them had communicated with the parents before their child started school. Communiqués ranged from a letter confirming entry, offering a welcome, or inviting a visit; to sheets, pamphlets and booklets giving details of uniform, forthcoming events, aims and aspirations. The quantity of notes sent home via the child varied from school to school; they advised parents about forthcoming events and the rising cost of school meals; they appealed for funds; they warned about health and safety; they invited parents in or they set restrictions on access.

But paper communications, though useful, do not necessarily increase understanding. One school sent home notes every week, including regular reminders that parents should not enter the school unless absolutely necessary. After three weeks, Wayne's mother was anxious to know how her son was getting on and plucked up courage to ask. The teacher, who was impressed by Wayne's outstanding ability, responded to the inquiry with a surprised, 'Why on earth do you ask?' The mother interpreted this to mean she had no right to ask and vowed never to go there again.

This example illustrates how easy it is for misunderstandings to occur and tenuous relationships to be nipped in the bud. Clearly, personal contacts are important. A month into the first term, parents said they would welcome discussions with staff on their child's progress and behaviour and how best they could help him. Yet they were reluctant to initiate such discussion themselves lest they seemed interfering. Teachers, on the other hand, did not express the same urgency to see the parents. They were equally divided between those who preferred to form their own opinions of the child and discover him for themselves; and those who would have liked more information on medical history or family background where these were thought to affect behaviour at school. There appeared to be a particular need for mutual understanding in schools with multi-ethnic intakes. Parents were not familiar with the British education system; teachers were not acquainted with the cultural habits of their pupils. A knowledge of ethnic customs combined with sensitive handling would have minimized distress among new entrants, especially at meals.

If we accept that mutual understanding is desirable, how best can it be achieved? Fringe participation and paper communications are neither necessary nor sufficient conditions for the development of parent-teacher relationships. Personal contact of a more than fleeting nature is essential. Creating opportunities for this after the child starts school may be too late. Mothers are already planning their futures and returning to work. After the early weeks they may no longer have the time, energy or inclination to visit the school. If positive relationships are to be established between parent and school, they must be begun before the child starts. One visit is not enough. To give parents an insight into what goes on in schools and staff the chance to get to know the parents, there needs to be a steady build-up of pre-entry visits over a period of several weeks. To avoid intolerable burdens on the teacher, this idea works best where entry is staggered so that there are not more than a few prospective entrants at one time. Freedom to visit any time avoids overcrowding in the classroom. In one school, four or five pre-entry visits were encouraged, increasing from an hour to a half-day. The success of this method depends on a willing staff who have confidence in what they are doing, and parents who are interested and cooperative.

Tizard, Mortimore and Burchell (1981) also argue that the period *before* the child starts school is a key time to establish contacts with parents, and recommend visits by teachers to parents and child at home, and 'clubs' for pre-schoolers and their mothers to attend at school.

Concluding remarks

Since parents are the primary educators of their children, it seems reasonable that requests for more knowledge of the school system should be met. In fact, at both the school and pre-school stages many parents wanted more first-hand knowledge of what their children were doing and direct invitations to help.

It is not clear how far parents' attitudes, anxieties and misapprehensions affect their child's transition to school. Some children seemed remarkably unaffected by their parents' worrying and fussing. But our study indicates that children who settled in with no apparent difficulty were more likely to have older siblings who had attended the school before them. Parents with long-standing connections with the school tended to express more positive attitudes, have more confidence in the staff and accept transition with equanimity. The presence of siblings at school, or at second-best older friends, was a powerful source of comfort to new entrants.

But the difficulties experienced by children in their early weeks at school may not always be resolved with the help of parents. When no siblings or friends are present, fear of the playground, of bigger children, of noise and crowds has ultimately to be overcome by the child himself and the sympathetic awareness of the staff. On the other hand, some problems could be avoided by greater understanding on either side. If parents saw the distress that some children suffered over school dinners they might make arrangements to let them come home in the early days. If staff were aware of the different cultural habits of their pupils they might be more tolerant, particularly at mealtimes. Ignorance of the aims and methods of infant education led a zealous mother to drill her daughter in the letters of the alphabet and counting to a hundred, which resulted in frustration for both child and teacher. Children who had had little or no pre-school experience were distressed by assembly in the hall, by noise and by restrictions on movement.

The study has shown, then, that the following points might be worth further consideration by everyone involved with children starting school:

- the family can be a powerful source of continuity and support particularly to children with older siblings in the school. Where none exists, substitutes may be found in the form of friends, neighbours, or pupils selected to look after new entrants.

- parental interest, where it exists, and the desire for more knowledge of what goes on in schools and pre-schools, might be maximized so that parents could support their children in an informed way.

- gaps in understanding might be bridged if parents and staff could have more insights into each other's worlds, both of which are inhabited by the child.

CHAPTER 8

First Day at School

'We are pleased to inform you that we will be able to admit your child on September 5th and we hope she will be very happy in our school.' Thus began the letter to Jane's parents from the head of her new infants school. But what will it be like for Jane as she comes into school for her first day? Will she indeed be 'happy'? We can only guess at what she feels as we observe her from the wings, perhaps recalling our own experiences of starting something new.

Admission and entry

Jane is already five. It is the policy in her area to admit children termly after their fifth birthday. There are variations on this: one school admits children in September and January but not at Easter; another encourages children to start on or soon after the day they are five; under-fives are admitted only at the head's discretion, in cases of special need or when staffing ratios permit. Local education authorities vary in their admission policies. In some areas, children are admitted the term in which they are five or even younger, but rising costs and cut-backs in staffing can make this policy hard to maintain. Under-fives start school in areas where there is only one annual intake, usually in September; if they are admitted in the school year in which they become five, new entrants can be as young as just turned four.

Depending on local policy, the age of new entrants to infant school can range from just four to five-and-a-half. This has implications for the length of time they have both in the infant department and at pre-school. Nursery staff told us that, while annual transfer was easier for them to cope with, transfer in the term he was five was best for the child. It is not clear whether starting age is related to the problems children can encounter. Our target children represented almost the entire range of ages and admission policies, yet young and old experienced some kind of difficulty. Probably more important than age is the degree of skill and sensitivity with which schools handle their new pupils.

Jane is starting school on the second day of term along with four other beginners. Entry procedures are largely a matter for the head teacher to decide and vary from school to school. Here is a selection from our sample:

New entrants all start together on the first day of term.

New entrants start in batches spread over several days or weeks.

New entrants start one at a time throughout the same day or week.

New entrants start one at a time throughout the year.

Classes vary according to the number of new entrants and the way they are grouped. Here are some of the possibilities:

The class consists entirely of new entrants and

a) builds up gradually during the first morning,

b) builds up gradually during the first few days or weeks,

c) builds up gradually throughout the year.

The class is already in existence, consisting of children who began one or two terms or years earlier; a small number of new entrants joins it each term and the oldest children move on.

Hours of attendance for beginners also vary from school to school. The range includes:

Full-time attendance from the beginning including staying to dinner.

Attending morning and afternoon but going home to dinner at first.

Attending mornings only for the first few days or until parents and staff agree that the child is ready for a full day.

For many children the transfer from pre-school means a major change in the length of time they are away from home. Sooner or later they must begin full-time attendance, which means starting school at approximately 9.00 a.m. and finishing around 3.00 p.m. Some children have been used to a longer day than this at day nursery or with a childminder, and the shorter hours create problems for working mothers who cannot be home in time to meet their youngsters. But for most children the school day is longer than that to which they have been accustomed, particularly if they have attended playgroups and nursery classes for half-days only. Nursery rest-time is seldom continued into school and fatigue is commonly reported among new entrants. Allowing them to come in the mornings only at first is one way schools cope with this problem; another is decreasing the length of the infant school day by dispensing with afternoon playtime or shortening the dinner break.

Arrival

'Today I'm going to school.' Jane is up early, eager to put on her new grey pinafore dress and red jumper. These are the clothes suggested by her head teacher and purchased from a local chain store. Many infant schools now adopt this practice. Her mother makes sure Jane has a substantial breakfast today, and instead of a leisurely look at the paper gets herself ready to take Jane to school.

On the way they pass the playgroup. It is nearly two months since Jane last went there. In fact, very few children enter school straight from pre-school; most of them have had a break of at least two weeks. The walk to school is longer for Jane but the route is familiar to her because, like most of our target children, she has visited the school before: on special occasions when her older brother was a pupil there and more recently when she was invited to see her new class. While most schools arrange for parents and children to visit before entry, a few also invite local day nursery and playgroup staff to bring prospective pupils too. In some cases the head deems a visit to be unnecessary especially where most of the children are transferring from the school's own nursery class.

Jane and her mother have been asked to arrive at school at 9.30 a.m. This means that the rest of the school are already settled and the head is able to greet each new pupil on arrival. First, they are taken to the secretary who checks Jane's address and telephone number. Jane's name is then ceremonially entered in the admissions register and she is given a name badge to wear for the morning. This ceremony is designed to help the child feel she now belongs to the school. The head personally escorts Jane and her mother to her classroom, holding Jane's hand all the way and chatting pleasantly. She introduces her to the teacher who greets Jane warmly and shows her a peg on which to hang her coat. The peg has Jane's name on it and a picture of a horse to help her identify it. At this point, her mother kisses Jane goodbye and leaves, saying she will be back at 12 o'clock. The teacher talks to Jane softly and unhurriedly, oblivious of the other 15 children present who are busy with tasks. She shows Jane around the classroom, then settles her at a table with a picture to colour. Five minutes later another new entrant arrives.

Jane's induction into school was pleasantly calm, well-organized and trouble-free. It contained four ingredients to make her arrival smooth:
Children were admitted one at a time.
The existing class was already settled.
The atmosphere was calm and quiet.
The child was given personal attention, made to feel she mattered and that the teacher had plenty of time for her.
Contrast this with Darren's arrival:
It is the first day of term. When the signal is given at 8.50 a.m. the infants line up to go into school. Among them are 40 new entrants and their parents. Inside, the corridors are teeming with children heading for their classrooms. The new arrivals are uncertain where to go. Eventually they find their way to the four reception rooms. Darren, with his mother, father and baby sister enter his classroom. His mother joins the queue to pay his dinner money to the teacher. Darren stands alone surveying the scene. Nine new entrants are gathered on the rug among bricks and construction toys. His mother approaches and he pushes her away. The teacher greets him, and his parents explain how he was used to being away at day nursery. Darren bursts into tears and resists the teacher's attempts to cuddle him. He kicks and shouts, and eventually his parents leave. He sits on the teacher's knee while she reads everyone a story. Gradually, his sobs subside and after 25 minutes he joins a group of boys building a tower.
There were three ingredients of Darren's induction which may have contributed to his unease:
A large number of new entrants were admitted together.
They arrived while the rest of the school were on the move and corridors congested.
The teacher was busy when they entered the classroom and could not give them personal attention till later.
But even in calm well-organized situations incidents can occur to upset the new arrival. Rosalie, seeing a brand new slide, eagerly ran to try it out and sustained a nasty fall; after much cuddling and comforting from her mother she recovered her composure and settled down. Eric, on the other hand, screamed so hysterically on his pre-entry visit that everyone feared the worst on his first day. As soon as his mother left, he made straight for a hollow play-cube and sat hidden inside it till he felt confident enough to come out and join the group.
Our 36 target children responded to their induction into infant school in one of four ways:

They settled in from the first with no apparent problems.
They showed distress initially but soon recovered.
They appeared to settle initially but showed distress later.
They showed distress initially and from time to time later.
These responses are discussed in this and the next two chapters.

Liaison and information

Like Jane, most children have set foot inside their new school before entry and some have already been introduced to their new teacher. But what does the teacher know of the child who is soon to be spending a third of his waking life with her? Two out of three teachers remembered seeing the child before. In one school, the reception teachers went to the nursery unit to see their prospective pupils, but the visit was so brief they failed to remember a single individual. Children who had been seen around the school with their older siblings were more likely to be remembered. Of those who came on a pre-entry visit, only half were specifically remembered by their teacher, the rest fading into obscurity. Perhaps the child is more likely to remember the teacher than the teacher the child.

Some reception teachers have no more than a vague idea which pre-school new entrants have attended, even when there is a nursery unit attached to their own school. We found that some of our sample schools had absolutely no contact with any pre-school provision in their area, nor did they want any. Others made contact either deliberately or incidentally. Incidental contacts occurred, for instance, when minders or playgroup helpers brought their own children to school and perhaps struck up an acquaintance with teacher or head. Deliberate contacts took the form of telephone calls, invitations to visit and informal discussions. These could be initiated by either side but more often were at the instigation of pre-school staff. For example, a nursery school head went each term to local infant schools to discuss briefly the children who were transferring; the matron of a day nursery asked local head teachers if her staff could bring groups of 'rising fives' to see their schools; and a playgroup leader, inspired by the project's study of continuity, decided to invite neighbouring primary school staff to watch her playgroup in session.

There are, of course, practical difficulties in exchanging visits between staff. Some head teachers, believing their role to be educators of parents as well as children, gave talks to parents at local playgroups explaining the purpose of play materials and giving hints on how best to help their child. This too has its problems since there are some pre-schools to which a head might not wish to be seen to lend approval.

Perhaps links between a school and its own nursery class or unit are the ones which are most easily taken for granted. Yet in some schools these are little more than a myth as far as the reception teacher is concerned. The most likely source of contact is the infant head who calls in from time to time. Depending on its location, the nursery is accessible to infant staff too, but sometimes invisible barriers seem to keep them away. Even that potential meeting place, the school staffroom, may be out-of-bounds to nursery staff, either because break times do not coincide or because of professional self-consciousness.

A teacher who is informed about her pupil's pre-school experience at least has a starting point for talking with him and will be able to avoid abortive attempts to question him about his 'play school'. It might be useful to know that he can handle paints and scissors, has had experience of being in a group and sharing an adult's attention. But many reception teachers do not wish to know these things or indeed anything about the child, preferring to regard him as a clean slate. They feel this has the advantage of allowing teacher and child to discover each other for themselves, unbiassed by the opinions of others.

More than half our sample schools received information about new entrants from the pre-schools and in most cases this was passed on to the reception teacher. But the information was limited and haphazard in availability and content. On the whole, very little was received from the playgroups unless informally by word of mouth. It was not usually asked for, being regarded by some heads as 'suspect'. A few local authority day nurseries made a point of sending a written report on each child, but it was not always clear what became of these. Staff in both playgroups and day nurseries expressed willingness to supply information if asked and regretted that their opinions were not valued more. Information from nursery education provisions tended to be of a more structured nature, particularly where the county's official record card for each child began at nursery age and was added to each year. This covered aspects like abilities and skills, language development and temperament. Even these were ignored by those teachers who wanted to form their own impressions of the child first.

Parents too had mixed feelings about the passing on of records, fearing that their child could be labelled to his detriment. They had no objections to records on progress and behaviour provided they had access to them.

They agreed that teachers should be forewarned about medical problems, but had reservations about divulging details of home background.

Every school requested a modicum of information from parents when their child started. First, his birth certificate was checked. Next, the parents completed an admission form with details of the child's names, address, telephone number, emergency contact, major illnesses and impairments. A few were also asked about pre-school experience but not in detail. Admission forms were usually available to the reception teacher if she wanted to see them.

It is thus with a minimum of information, if any, that the teacher greets the child on his first day at school and embarks on the delicate task of negotiating the teacher–pupil relationship.

Introductions

Jane's classroom is bright with pictures and books; in the corridor outside is a colourful display of berries and gourds against an orange drape. The picture on the drawer she is given matches the one on her peg. There is a book, pencil and crayons ready for her. The environment signals friendliness and welcome; it looks a pleasant place to be in. It is more likely to be so if it is not the first day back after the holidays when everything had to be taken down and packed away. Some teachers come in before the term starts to prepare an attractive setting for the children. Another put the opposite view; surrounded by bare walls she explained, 'I believe in concentrating on getting to know the children first'.

The environment may be intended by adults to convey specific messages, but we do not know how effective they are. One school with an eighty per cent immigrant population displayed in the entrance hall a collage of multi-ethnic faces with the caption 'Infants at Rose Street come from all over the world'. What does this mean to the dark-skinned boy who has come from just down the road? In another school, a reception class of Asians, Chinese and West Indians mounted a frieze of 'Our Portraits' in which the faces were cut out of pale *pink* card. The pictures in the reading scheme were all of white children. But do cultural anomalies like these matter? The coloured five-year-old may already identify with the white world outside his family. Sundar, a Ugandan Asian, resented his teacher because she was the only non-white member of staff. His nursery nurses had all been white and he complained to his mother, 'Why can't my teacher be the same as everyone else?'

The familiar adults of pre-school have been left behind; teacher and child have to get to know each other. Teachers have their own ways of trying to get the relationship off to a good start. Jane's teacher took her aside several times and spoke to her face-to-face, using eye contact and facial expressions to establish positive bonds with her. Some teachers use physical contact, taking the child by the hand or putting an arm around him.

Addressing the child by name is very important; the wise teacher also finds out the correct way to pronounce it and uses the form to which the child is accustomed, such as Penny instead of Penelope. Besides giving new entrants a name badge to wear, some teachers make a game of remembering names: badges are covered up and children have to guess each others' names. Registration can also be used to encourage children to respond to their own names and to learn each others. The register is marked every session as a record of attendance. It could be the child's first group experience in his new class. Jane's teacher called Christian names only and did not worry if some failed to reply audibly. Other teachers make it into a more formal occasion. The children are expected to sit still and attentive, and to respond with a clear 'Yes, Mrs Brook'. Many children have already made the acquaintance of 'register time' at playgroup or nursery where it often forms part of a conscious attempt to train children in listening and responding.

In group situations like this children react with varying degrees of shyness or showing-off. Some appear overwhelmed and self-conscious, remaining silent at first. One teacher feels she should try to draw these children out; another prefers to leave them alone to look on. Some children are bumptious and over-confident; they behave inappropriately in group situations, talking loudly when everyone else is quiet or, like Ian, rushing forward to switch off the school television broadcast because he did not like the noise. But formal group time is a powerful mechanism for social control. Inappropriate behaviour meets not only with rebuke from the teacher but the tacit disapproval of everyone present. Sooner or later even the most unabashed new entrant is obliged to conform. The embarrassment which can be incurred by an individual in group situations is a potent weapon in the hands of a teacher who wants to shame a child in front of his peers. But the skilful teacher can also save the new entrant's face by showing herself to be on his side: 'He's not really crying, that's just a noise he's making.'

Tone of voice is particularly important, whether the teacher is addressing an individual or the whole class. When another pupil needs a firm reprimand it is not easy to avoid upsetting a sensitive newcomer, and in the early days parents are regaled with tales of naughty children and angry teachers. Some schools are remarkably peaceful, free from the loud signal systems and commanding adult voices which abound in others. Several target children burst into tears when shouted at, or were distressed by sudden strange loud noises.

Children vary tremendously in the amount of reassurance they need and teachers vary in their willingness to give it. While some staff believe the child should be encouraged to be as independent as possible, others coax him along with lavish praise, hugs of approval and the occasional Smartie. Some teachers are especially aware of the child's need to find support among his peers, encouraging children to chat among themselves and make friends. By contrast one teacher, overhearing her new pupils talking in Gujarati, tapped them smartly on the heads and told them to speak English. Experienced teachers involve the whole class in supporting the newcomers. Beginners are introduced by name, existing pupils are asked to look after them and sometimes are paired with them for the day. Pairing can be a very successful way of eliminating minor anxieties and distress in new entrants. It works best in classes which are vertically grouped: the new child is introduced to an older classmate who shows him where to go and what to do.

Explanations

From time to time Jane's teacher paused to explain personally to her what was going to happen next. But most of our target children entered school with a number of other beginners and explanations were given to the group or even the whole class. On the first day there is a great deal for the newcomer to take in and the sheer volume of talk coming from the teacher is impressive. Even the most sensitive explanations are fraught with new words peculiar to school: home base, plimsolls, shoe bag, dinner lady. We saw bewilderment greet glib commands like 'line up' and 'not more than four at the sandtray'. We observed baffled expressions at ambiguous questions like 'What do you want to say?' (meaning 'What do you want me to write under your picture?') and 'Where do you think this feather came from?' (eventual answer: 'The gutter'.)

One or two teachers took the new entrants on a tour of the school, showing them where everything was and introducing them to key figures on the way: 'This is Mrs Wells who cooks our lovely dinners' and 'This is where we come to see Mrs Neal if we have an accident'. The mysteries of the dark alcove in the corridor and that something called 'The Hall' were revealed. Throughout the trip the teacher answered questions and gave explanations: what the fire extinguisher is for, why the fishtank is bubbling, why the urinal makes such a loud noise.

Arrangements for going to the toilet can cause difficulties. In schools where the toilets are a long way from the classrooms, visiting them becomes something of a ceremony. At appointed times the children line up and are escorted to the toilets and back again. This is not only time-consuming but means that the child must go at the required time whether he wants to or not; otherwise he has to be taken specially. He may worry about this and be afraid to ask; if he has an accident he loses face in front of strangers. Fortunate are the children in modern or adapted premises with facilities close at hand; easy access means they can go without having to ask. Some children were perturbed by the unfamiliarity, the smell or the lack of privacy. Not all of them were capable of managing themselves and one embarrassed child emerged with his trousers around his ankles. Another was mystified by the teacher's constant use of the word 'lavatory' instead of toilet or loo. Hand-washing arrangements were also diverse; there was the novelty of pressing taps instead of turning them and the fascination of water running into an open drain under the basins. All these things were carefully explained by teachers who were able to see things through the eyes of a child.

Introducing work tasks

The first task Jane was given to do was to draw a picture of her house and colour it in. When she had finished, the teacher would write some words beneath it for her to trace over. Most of our target children's first tasks were like this. Some teachers had set out a selection of toys and apparatus for the children to choose from when they first arrived, in a similar way to playgroup or nursery. But sooner or later they were introduced to 'work', that is, a specific task usually related to literacy or numeracy, which they were expected to complete and have checked. The task was introduced variously with the words: 'Would you like to?' or 'I would like you to', but either way the child had no option. If a child demurred, two attitudes prevailed: one which said we all have to do things we don't want to do; the other, that it's all right this time but in future you will have to do it. Teachers with vertically grouped classes expected new entrants to start work straightaway because if they were allowed to play the older children would want to do the same. Most of the parents said that children of this age should start 'working'.

Most of the target children settled to their work with a will, as if pleased to have something positive and productive to do. They required frequent short bouts of encouragement and approval. In order to get it, new children ignored queues and went straight to the teacher for immediate attention. For the first few days they usually received it. One or two children, having completed part of a task, did not know what to do next and would sit and wait idly as if afraid to move until told.

Children responded to work tasks in different ways. Penny burst into tears every time work was mentioned; the teacher resolved this by pretending that everything was an activity to be chosen. Rosalie was bossy and over-confident and frequently sought adult approval by telling tales; the teacher discouraged this by pretending not to hear. Ian was unable to sit still for long and kept fooling around under the table to the annoyance of his companions; the teacher removed him to a place beside her desk. Nadia, who could count to a hundred, was disgusted when told to copy the figures one to five; her teacher resolved the clash by promising her a hundred beads to thread on a string if she could complete her work first.

Children's initial attempts require sensitive treatment. The concept of work brings with it the notion of getting it right and the child learns how to succeed. . . . or fail. Pippa, who had painstakingly coloured a purple teddy, was told scathingly, 'Bears aren't purple'. Sunil, unable to hold his pencil 'properly', was repeatedly told he was stupid. By contrast, most teachers lavishly praised even the sketchiest efforts: 'That's lovely Debbie, you can show all the children'.

Failure may be learnt in a more subtle way. Schools vary in the work materials they give to new entrants. Some target children were delighted to be handed an exercise book with plain pages on which to write and draw. Others were given paper at first and only acceded to a book on reaching a certain standard of neatness. There seemed little incentive though for the boy who was given scraps of computer paper long after everyone else had a book.

The ability of new entrants to cope with work tasks varied considerably, ranging from those who could scarcely control a pencil to those who were soon drawing small pictures with neatly copied words beneath them. This kind of ability seemed to be related, not only to pre-school experience, but to the availability at home of suitable materials with which to have practised.

When tasks were finished, children were usually allowed to choose from a limited selection of activities. The new entrants responded to this in different ways. Celia, who had come straight from home, seemed unable to decide what to do and wandered aimlessly about. Most of the target children had been used to choice at pre-school, but nonetheless reacted with varying degrees of uncertainty and apathy. Melanie sat for 20 minutes beside a construction set and built nothing; Wayne looked absently on at the others; Ruth kept asking if it was dinnertime and Sundar if it was home time. Paul and Jenny decided to get acquainted and the following conversation was overheard:

Jenny: I'm bigger than you. I'm four.

Paul: I'm four.

Jenny: Look, I'm bigger than you (moving to compare her height with his).

Paul: If you're four and I'm four, we're both the same size.

Introducing specific activities

Milk time

When this study was taking place, it was the practice for children in infant schools to be given free milk daily. This came in bottles or cartons holding one-third of a pint. The milk was drunk through a straw. Children who had attended a pre-school had already been accustomed to drinks and biscuits being dispensed with more or less ceremony. Milk or squash was usually drunk from beakers. The reception teacher has to show new entrants how to make a hole in the milk-top and how to use a straw. She has to cope with spills, smashed bottles and leaky containers.

Milk time is treated as a specific event in some classes and passes almost unnoticed in others. Here are examples:

Milk is available on a table, each bottle labelled with a child's name. Children help themselves and replace the empty bottle in the crate. Drinking time is flexible: any time during the morning.

The children go a few at a time to the class 'shop' and buy a bottle of milk with toy money: milk 2p, straw 1p, a mat to stand the bottle on 2p.

The whole class are gathered on the rug. The teacher names a colour and children who are wearing it fetch their milk. Drinking time is used for the discussion of news.

Target children responded to milk time in different ways. Although it was not compulsory, one or two children built up a dislike of milk which put them off going to school. Some behaved inappropriately, walking about when they were expected to sit down to drink, handing the empty bottle to the teacher or leaving half the milk. Others were very slow and did not know what to do if the straw bent. One child asked for hot milk. Milk time was usually followed by playtime, which is discussed in detail in the next chapter.

Assembly

Assembly is a gathering together of all or part of the school to worship God. For practical reasons it is usually held in the school hall. It occurs at the start of the day or at some time during the morning, more rarely in the afternoon. The nursery class may be included once a week or less. Parents are sometimes invited, either regularly or on special occasions. The assembly may be conducted by the head, a member of staff or a class. For any one child it may occur daily or less. It lasts from about ten to thirty minutes. It usually consists of one or two hymns, a prayer and a talk. In multi-ethnic areas the content is sometimes adapted to be more appropriate. In addition to the religious content, it may also be used as an opportunity to celebrate birthdays, to launch appeals, to award praise and blame, and to reiterate school rules.

A new entrant's first assembly must be handled carefully. Removing the child from the comparative familiarity of his classroom and putting him with a large number of strangers in strange surroundings can cause extreme discomfort. Celia (see Chapter 13) had been in school only ten minutes when her class went into assembly and the shock caused her distress which lasted for weeks. Other target children were more fortunate: assembly was either postponed till later in the morning or for several days. The following concessions to new entrants were observed:

Reception classes had a shorter assembly in one of their classrooms and were gradually introduced to school assembly in the hall after half term. The children were taught the words of some of the hymns beforehand. The class teacher went into assembly with them and stayed close by. Lively music was playing as the youngsters entered.

The children sat on the floor instead of standing in rows.

The head introduced them by name and encouraged the older children to be kind to them.

Most new entrants conformed to expected standards of quiet and orderly behaviour. Inappropriate behaviours, such as talking aloud and interrupting the head's talk with a piece of personal information, were short-lived. Since the youngest pupils were usually positioned at the front, they could not resist the temptation to turn around; there was a fair amount of fidgeting and shuffling. When uncertain what to do, they copied the older children.

Physical education

This refers to that period of physical activity when the children use specific apparatus and movements to promote muscular coordination and agility. It usually takes place in the hall, though in fine weather portable apparatus can be taken outside. Again, it needs to be introduced sensitively to the new entrant, with careful explanations. Even its name 'Pee Yee', can be mystifying. Physical activity of this nature, for reasons of health and safety, requires special clothing such as plimsolls and shorts or pants. The removal of extraneous clothing can cause the beginner acute embarrassment and insecurity, and some children adamantly refuse to be parted from their clothes. In addition, the teacher may find herself inundated with requests to fasten zips, buckles and bows. The following strategies were employed to make the introduction to PE more smooth: new entrants were taken to the hall to watch another class in action; the teacher gave a commentary on the different pieces of apparatus and the purpose of the procedures; beginners were given the option of joining in at first.

Reactions were on the whole favourable, the children entering into activities with obvious enjoyment. Distress centred mainly around dressing and undressing: one child persistently refused to put his plimsolls on and the teacher remedied this by assisting him with her shoehorn. Alan was horrified when told to change saying, 'But everyone will see me'; the teacher resolved this by explaining that all the other children would be undressing too. Ruth was terrified of being last because she could not do up her shoe; another child was asked to stay and help her.

Music and movement sessions were similarly dealt with and all the children appeared to enjoy them.

Going home

As the morning drew to an end, teachers employed various closing procedures; clearing up the classroom was popularly followed by a gathering of the children together for a story or discussion. This was sometimes taken as an opportunity to reiterate the morning's events. It was during this time, when the child was sitting passively, that signs of fatigue became apparent: rubbing eyes, looking glazed, yawning, stretching, keeping close to the teacher. This occurred regardless of pre-school experience and was doubtless due to the bombardment of new stimuli. By the time new entrants were putting their coats on, parents were already gathering outside. Children who were staying all day prepared for dinner (see Chapter 10) and the rest were going home. Over-anxious mothers filtered into the classrooms to confront weary teachers and it was then that communication gaps were exposed: the Indian mother who asked if her daughter had learned all she was supposed to received the exasperated reply that the child is only expected to do as she is told; the working mum who was concerned about being late to fetch her son was told that schools are for education, not babysitting. But on the whole it had been a good morning. Jane's habit of sucking two fingers whenever she was unoccupied had been noticeably absent and most children went off chatting happily. Minor hitches were soon dealt with: it's the shoebag and not your shoes that must stay in school; your coat hasn't really been stolen, you're looking at the wrong peg; the pencil is really yours to keep in your drawer. 'Goodbye, see you tomorrow'.

What next?

Some children who coped happily with the first day were less enthusiastic when they found they had to go to school every day. Even children who had attended a day nursery full-time cried to go back there. Firm handling by parents and sensitive treatment by teachers overcame this kind of reluctance in a few days. But distress was triggered in some apparently settled children by a period of absence or an accident in the early weeks. Tracey fell down in PE and refused to go to school on PE days; Sally's school was closed when the heating oil ran out, and her former boldness changed to apathy; children who had been away started crying at playtime and dinnertime. Some beginners were upset by disturbances at home: Eric started crying in the mornings after his father went into hospital. The effects of such disruptions in the life of the new entrant could last at least until we ceased to observe him after six weeks at school.

Our target children will remain in their reception class for a term, a year or even for the whole of their infant career. During this time the majority of teachers will keep records of their progress. Additionally, they might also note relevant information on family, health, speech, behaviour and personality. Record forms are used, often supplemented by written notes. In all cases these will be passed on to the next teacher or school. Occasionally, examples of the child's work will also be included. About half the children will have the opportunity to visit the next class with their teacher before moving on. Around the age of eight their infant days will be over and they will transfer to the junior or middle school.

Summary remarks

While some children settled into school with no apparent difficulty, including one child who had also moved house five days earlier, the majority of target children showed signs of bewilderment, fatigue or distress, especially on the first day.

Particular sources of difficulty were:
- arriving during noise and bustle or in a hurry
- bewilderment at unfamiliar words and questions
- being bombarded with new information
- sudden loud noises, such as the school's signal system
- teacher's tone of voice
- the shock of strange situations away from the classroom, such as assembly, playtime, and dinnertime (see also Chapters 9 and 10)
- unfamiliar toilet arrangements
- undressing for PE
- fear of being last or left behind
- losing face in front of others
- apprehension about work tasks and the possibility of failure
- uncertainty about what to do next
- missing mother, friends or pre-school

Distress could be triggered by an accident or by a period of absence.

The key to smooth transition seems to lie in avoiding the shock of anything *sudden* in the way of sights, sounds or experiences, and in introducing everything *gradually* in an atmosphere of unhurried calm.

The following strategies are recommended for use in school:

- staggered entry with a personal welcome for mother and child
- a calm and unhurried start after the rest of the school is settled
- being prepared for the new entrant, having his things ready with his name on
- calling him by name and getting it right
- having a point of contact to begin a conversation with him
- having plenty of time for him, making him feel he matters
- allowing him the opportunity to look on at others from a secluded vantage point
- having foreknowledge of his particular problems
- being supportive of him in front of the other children and sparing him embarrassment
- encouraging other children to be supportive and kind
- pairing him with older children
- giving him lots of reassurance and praise
- explaining things carefully as they occur
- reducing loud commands and signal systems to a minimum
- giving him opportunities to make friends among his classmates
- explaining unfamiliar words and phrases
- showing him around and introducing him to other staff he will meet
- recognizing his need for frequent short bursts of attention
- placing him where he can watch older children in assembly
- letting him watch other children doing PE and getting changed
- make use of other children to help him get dressed or use scissors
- encourage him with a smart new set of work materials
- allow him a mid-morning drink or snack to combat fatigue
- be extra sensitive to his reactions after a period of absence or a disturbance in his home life

The following additional hints are offered to parents:

- give your child a good breakfast and an unhurried start to the day
- have school-type pencils, crayons and scissors at home for him to practise with if he wants to
- don't be over-anxious and harass the teacher when collecting your child for the first time, see how he is tomorrow
- send him to school as regularly as possible

CHAPTER 9

Playtime

The notion of 'playtime' represents a major discontinuity in the experience of most children starting school. Playtime is largely a feature of the primary school where it has a distinctive nature rarely encountered in pre-school settings.

The expression play *time* suggests what it usually is, a specific period set aside for the purpose of playing. Infant school playtimes are usually ten or fifteen minutes in length and occur during the morning and, in many schools, during the afternoon sessions also. The epithet *play* time suggests that activities during this period are distinct from the rest of the session to which traditionally the notion of 'work' adhered. Today the concepts of work and play in school are not so sharply defined but the use of the term 'playtime' persists. School playtimes represent breaks in the programme. They usually occur at fixed regular times.

The occurrence of a formalized timetabled break of this nature is seldom found in pre-schools. The concept of play is a flexible one and is not clearly distinguished from other forms of activity. In fact, many practitioners hold the view that all the activities are a form of play through which the children learn.

The play setting

For the sample children in this study, playtime represented a totally new experience. They were required to go at appointed times beyond the bounds of their new classrooms into the hitherto unexplored world of the school playground. Each playground encompassed a wider territory and a greater number of bodies than encountered in any of their pre-schools.

The play space

Every infant school has its playground, though there is considerable variety in size, shape and type. In some schools, particularly older ones, the playground is simply a rectangular space with a hard surface. In others the play space comprises a hard tarmac area with additional stretches of grass or tree-studded patches of hard earth. Most of the sample play areas were flat, though one or two had raised grassy banks. A few schools also possessed borders of shrubs or flowers. Grassed areas ranged from small lawns to sports fields and a few included a swimming pool.

Availability is largely dependent on the weather. On rainy days the children may not be able to go outside at all and schools have their own ways of coping with this; in some, classroom activities continue uninterrupted for the whole session, while in others a break is taken and although the children remain in the classroom, they are allowed to choose an activity or read comics. After rain and particularly in winter, grassed and earth areas are out-of-bounds for practical and safety reasons and only the tarmac area can be used.

The play area may have to accommodate at one time any number of children ranging from one class or one year-group to the whole school. Play areas in the study ranged from a square courtyard enclosed on all sides by the two-storey school building to a large unbounded campus of irregular shape.

Contrast these with the child's previous experience of playspace. This may have been no more than his day-to-day play in his own back garden, the street outside his home or trips to the local park. But for some children even these opportunities for outdoor play are ruled out. Not every home has a garden or suitable playing space outside. Children at home with parents or with minders may be confined to upstairs flats with little or no opportunity for going out. One such minder lived on the third floor of a high-rise block. The toddlers sometimes played on the walkway outside her front door. But games of bat and ball were short-lived, the ball soon disappearing over the balustrade or down the steps. Dinky cars and other small toys quickly vanished into a neighbouring garbage heap or down one of the drainage holes in the floor.

Many playgroups (27 per cent of those sampled) have no facilities for outdoor play. Those in private homes may have a garden, but many playgroups meet in halls with perhaps a car park or grassy field outside. The playgroup leader may deem this area fit for play only in the summer months or consider it unsuitable or unsafe at all times. In one case a leader, at first appalled by the wild state of the field outside the hut, decided to turn it to advantage and the long grass became a paradise for imaginative play. Another playgroup was situated in a modern well-appointed playroom annexed to the parish church. Its garden was the churchyard and the children played happily on apparatus carefully sited between the gravestones. Occasionally playgroups are found in community centres with purpose-built playrooms and gardens, but more usually playgroup leaders have to make the best use of what there is. This may mean putting out a row of chairs to define the permitted play area, screening off hazards such as piles of waste and rubble and creating a makeshift boundary. Boundaries can be a problem and staff sometimes require ingenuity to devise ways of making the outside safe, a problem not confined to playgroups since the grounds of some schools are not continuously fenced. Boundaries are essential for the security and safety of young children and for the peace of mind of those in charge of them.

It was the nursery schools, nursery units and local authority day nurseries in our sample who were best provided with outdoor play space. Most of them had a garden which was exclusively for their own children's use. They had grassed and hard areas, and many also boasted a covered patio which was a boon in poor weather. Many of these gardens contained trees and shrubs and, in a few, the children were allowed to participate in the gardening. One nursery school was particularly memorable: the garden was a delight, consisting of large shady lawns and herbaceous borders threaded with winding paths along which the children could embark on intricate journeys with their trikes and trucks. The gardener was one of the mothers.

Play equipment and amenities

Most, but not all, school playgrounds used by new entrants contained at least one fixed piece of climbing apparatus, most commonly of tubular metal in various forms. Sometimes concrete structures suitable for gross motor activities were provided and these took the form of steam engines, tunnels, waves, zig-zags and stepping stones. Tree stumps and logs were observed to a lesser extent and their use usually limited to dry weather. In some schools the fixtures were available to all children while in others there was a rota for each class to take a turn.

Fixed apparatus was also much in evidence in nursery schools and day nurseries where it was often complemented by swings. Most of these provisions also had a sandpit and some a built-in paddling pool, but comparatively few playgroups and childminders possessed outdoor fixed equipment of any kind. The gardens of minders are of course as varied as gardens everywhere and minded children may be fortunate in sharing a well-equipped family's toys, but for many minders the expense of providing large apparatus is too great. For playgroups too, expense is often a problem, but for those in rented huts and halls there is also the fact that any outdoor space that might be available is not exclusively for their own use; thus fixed equipment might be impractical or vulnerable.

Many pre-schools, with or without fixed apparatus, provide toys which can be taken outside and put away again. The life of the staff is made considerably easier if there are storage facilities which are easily accessible to the play area, and lack of a suitable store is another difficulty which besets many playgroups. Equipment which can be used outdoors includes wheeled toys such as trucks, trolleys, tricyles, cars and prams; rockers, slides and small climbing frames; tents and paddling pools; and portables like tyres, wooden blocks, barrels and crates. A well-equipped pre-school also provides balls, rings, beanbags, ropes and hoops. And in good weather the garden may become an extension of indoors with sand- and waterplay, painting, woodwork and junk. But wheeled and portable equipment of this kind is rarely seen in infant school playgrounds at playtime. In the one or two places where any was observed it was confined to the reception classes and their environs. Most schools discouraged toys brought from home, though a few allowed balls to be brought and in these cases there was usually a special area set aside for ball games. A small number of schools brightened their playground floors with painted lines, footprints and hopscotch mark-outs. Physical comfort was sometimes provided for with a couple of garden seats or benches and occasionally a drinking fountain, but these amenities were missing from many playgrounds.

The playground setting, then, can represent several discontinuities in the experience of a child starting school. First, he may have had little or no outdoor play at his pre-school whereas now it forms part of his daily routine. Second, the play area is almost certainly larger than any he encountered at pre-school. Third, play equipment, if available, will be different in both quantity and type from what he has been used to.

Playtime procedures

All the schools attended by the sample children had regular daily play-times. Every school had a morning playtime but in some schools the afternoon one had been dispensed with in favour of a shorter session. Except in bad weather outdoor play was compulsory for all children; only in exceptional circumstances could individuals stay in.

The purpose of playtime was never made explicit but clearly there were specific intentions for its use: that in this ten or fifteen minute span the staff should take a break with a cup of tea or coffee, and that the children should take a break to let off steam, eat a snack and go to the toilet. In a sense it was 'free' time, but the freedom was prescribed. Compare this with the pre-schools. Outdoor play, where available, occurred on a much more flexible basis. In all cases indoor and outdoor play were available concurrently and children had a choice. Some would always avail them-selves of an opportunity to go out whereas others rarely if ever ventured beyond the bounds of the playroom. The length of outdoor playtime varied considerably. In one day nursery the children could be out all day if they chose, coming in only for meals and story time. In some playgroups and nursery classes the outside area was made available for set periods for those who wanted it. In all cases where outdoor play was available it was for considerably longer than ten or fifteen minutes.

The formalization of school playtime usually means that large numbers of children are moving from classrooms to play area at the same time. To enable them to proceed safely and smoothly there and back again schools adopt a variety of strategies. The choice of strategy depends on the number of children involved, the layout of the building and the proximity of the play area as well as on professional attitudes to order and organi-zation.

The beginning of playtime may be signalled to the whole school by bell, buzzer or hooter. For a new entrant the noise emitted by some of these devices can be a strange and baffling experience. On the other hand, teachers may rely on their own clocks and watches. Going out to play may involve a ritual of lining up at the classroom door, waiting for a degree of silence, then proceeding in file through the building to its exit. Or an informal approach may be adopted: around the appointed time, the teacher tells the children they can go out as soon as they have finished the task in hand. For children starting school in the winter, playtime brings the added routine of fetching their coat, putting it on and coping with buttons. For the teacher too, helping children on and off with their outer wear can occupy most of her breaktime in the early days. Here are some examples of children in different schools going out to play.

Rosalie:
lives in a flat without a garden. At playgroup she preferred indoor activities and rarely went outside.

She is a confident little girl who loves to please. She has been at school a week now and the class is gathered in the story corner for discussion time. The atmosphere is relaxed.

Five minutes before playtime the teacher reminds the children about orderly behaviour. 'Why do I want you to walk and not run?' 'Because it is dangerous' replies Rosalie with her usual confidence. There are flurries of snow in the air and the children are told to put on their coats. The cloakroom is an integral part of the reception unit and the teacher spends several minutes helping with buttons and zips. Rosalie competently changes from plimsolls into buckled shoes and draws the teacher's attention to a boy who cannot do up his shoes. Then she buttons her coat and puts on her fur bonnet, upside down. She then turns to help another girl, Susan. The teacher says, 'You may go out to play when you are ready.' Rosalie replies, 'I'm ready but I'll wait for Susan.' She eventually strolls out to play hand in hand with a little group of girls.

Rosalie's was a modern single-storey first school with the reception unit set apart down a pleasant path.

Contrast procedures there with this large urban school which is in a two-storey building housing infant and junior departments.

Sundar:
It is his second day at school. The children are gathered on the rug in the story corner looking at books. Suddenly the calm is shattered by a piercing shriek. Some of the children jump. Sundar looks mystified. No one explains that the noise is the school hooter.

Nothing happens, so presumably the signal was intended for the junior school upstairs. A few minutes later another shriek rends the air. This time the teacher responds. 'Line up at the door Class Two.' The children make their way towards the classroom door. Some of them are old hands having been at school a week. Others, like Sundar, are still bemused by the strangeness of it all. At his day nursery he spent most of the day pleasing himself whether he played indoors or out.

'I want a straight line,' exhorts the teacher standing at the open door. Sundar appears not to hear and wanders out through the door oblivious of her calls. But once in the long corridor he cannot remember the way to the playground and drifts along with the stream of children pouring from another classroom. Unfortunately they are heading for the hall. Sundar looks confused and his eyes fill with tears. After a few moments a passing teacher notices him and points him in the right direction. He goes into the playground and stands looking dazed. Then he joins the queue for the slide.

For some children, a school day punctuated by such sets of procedures for going out becomes confusing and they lose track of time. This is what happened to one such child.

Ian:
He has been at school for three weeks now, a lively sociable child who loves playtime. His playgroup which he attended once a week had no outdoor play space and Ian used to dissipate his energy by zooming round and round the playroom in his favourite pedal car.
Now it is mid-afternoon and the class are clearing up their activities. Then they can go to their pegs in the corridor outside to fetch their coats. Ian spends a long time chatting and eventually returns clad in an anorak with the zip undone. The class wait in their seats to be dismissed group by group. Ian puts his head down and rubs his arm back and forth across the table. Because he is fidgeting his group is the last to be dismissed.
At last Ian roars joyfully out through the door, then stops in surprise. 'It's playtime!' he exclaims. 'I thought it was time to go 'ome.'

Once outside there are certain rules to be kept in the interests of safety and good management. Children may not run back and forth to the classroom without permission or leave the premises. They may or may not be allowed to bring snacks or toys to school. Where snacks are permitted they may be restricted to certain items like apples and crisps to discourage dental decay, and wrappers are expected to be put in the bin. Where play equipment is available there may for safety reasons be limitations on its use.

The end of playtime entails certain organizational procedures and again these vary from school to school. A regular pattern is adhered to and soon learned by the new entrants. The pattern consists of two parts: signalling the end of play and returning to the classroom. The same pattern obtains in many schools at the beginning of each session also.

The signal for the end of play is usually auditory, such as a bell, buzzer or whistle. Often there are two signals, each with a specific meaning: stand still; line up. Less common is the visual signal such as the class teacher positioning herself at a given spot to meet her pupils, or number or colour cards held up.

Here are examples of end-of-play procedures observed in seven schools. They range from informal to formal.

School 1.

A first school with eight classes, children aged five to eight.

The end of play is marked by the arrival of class teachers who stand near the entrance to the building. The reception teacher stands at the top of the path leading to the reception unit which is set apart from the main building. The children gather around their teachers and are escorted back to their own rooms.

School 2.

A combined first and middle school with four classes, children aged five to 12.

A handbell is rung. The school is small and the classrooms are near the playground. Children move off individually to their own classrooms using three different entrances.

School 3.

A first school with eight classes, children aged five to eight. Teacher on duty blows a whistle and all children stand still. Teacher blows the whistle again and all the children move off individually but in the same direction towards the building. There is only one entrance. Head and reception teachers stand just inside to guide new entrants.

School 4.

An infant school with eight classes, children aged five to seven. Teacher on duty blows whistle and children gather on one of the tarmac areas. Teacher holds up colour cards. Each class is named after a specific colour and when they recognize their own colour they go to their classroom.

School 5.

A primary school. The three infant classes take their playtime first, children aged five to seven. Teacher on duty blows whistle and children stand still. Teacher blows whistle again and children proceed to their own classrooms which have entrances directly from the playground. Each class lines up outside the classroom door until their teacher arrives.

School 6.
A combined first and middle school. The eight first school classes, children aged five to eight, take their playtime after the others.
Handbell is rung. Teacher on duty blows a whistle and children line up in classes at one end of the playground.
They wait until their own teacher arrives to escort them back to their classroom.

School 7.
An infant school with 12 classes, children aged five to seven in a very large playground.
Handbell is rung. Children form a single line near the building's entrance. Some children have been standing there ready for some time. The single line is very long and winds like a snake across the play-ground. The two teachers on duty escort the children in through one entrance. Children proceed along the corridors to their own classrooms. To new entrants the corridors look alike and in the early days some find themselves in the wrong classrooms.

After some initial confusion new entrants soon become familiar with these routines. Probably their greatest difficulty is with the notion of 'lining up.' Some children appeared completely baffled when on their first morning at school they were told to 'make a line'. . . . But at least one playgroup leader was observed instructing the children in lining up, as part of her programme for what she called 'preparing them for school.'

The people in the playground

Perhaps one of the biggest discontinuities in the play experience of a school entrant is the presence of a large number of children and a small proportion of adults.

The relationship between the size of the play space and the number of children using it has important consequences for the young child in terms of density and noise. The smaller or more reticent child avoids the hurly burly by lingering on the fringes or seeking the refuge of a wall or seat. From being one of the oldest at his pre-school the new entrant is now among the youngest. Our sample children shared playgrounds with boys and girls of up to seven, eight and twelve years of age.

The presence of siblings or friends is a comfort to new entrants. Of the children observed, all those who had older brothers or sisters in the playground at the same time sought them out on the first day and continued to do so throughout the early weeks. The friends of these older siblings also became their playmates. Where no siblings were present, the sample children sought out older friends and neighbours whom they already knew. Youngsters who knew no one at all tended to stand around and look on at the rest. The twins in the sample exhibited rather different behaviour, at first deliberately avoiding each other in the playground. After receiving rebuffs from some of the older children, they sought each other's company to such an extent that during the early weeks they were scarcely apart. Another child, Rosalie, approached playtime with apparent confidence, soon taking delight in organizing a group of her classmates. However, her enthusiasm turned to lethargy after being repeatedly teased by older children about her fur hat. The presence of older children in the same play area is not always disadvantageous. In one school practical use was made of it; each new entrant was paired for playtime with an older child from his own vertically grouped class. For the two sample children who had no siblings in this school, pairing proved very successful and both girls accepted the playground situation with equanimity.

For two children observed in another school the segregation of the new entrants from the rest into a small playground of their own proved distressing. This school admitted a new intake of nearly a hundred children at the beginning of the year and for the first week or two they spent their playtimes in an inner courtyard surrounded on all sides by the two-storey building. There was an ample supply of play equipment and supervision. The play area was small and crowded, and its enclosed nature amplified the noise. Although Sundar and Priti had attended the same day nursery full-time for several years they did not seek each other's company at school. At first, in common with many other children there, they stood around or sat on a low wall looking on. When any of these children were crying or in need of comfort for some reason, they received no solace from the other children who were also new and who simply stared at them. This situation changed dramatically when they joined the older pupils in the main playground. Both Sundar and Priti made a beeline for older children with whom they were friends out of school and from then on playtime became a happier experience for both of them.

In pre-school situations children playing outside rarely find themselves with more than forty other children and, because of the optional nature of indoor-outdoor play, this number is often much less. None of the sample children attended a pre-school of more than 45 children. In their respective school playgrounds numbers ranged from 70 to 380.

The ratio of available adults is also likely to be much lower at school. The majority of schools use a rota system for members of staff to take turns at supervising the play area. This is usually on a daily or weekly basis. Depending on the size and shape of the area and the number of children using it there will be one, two or even three supervisors. For the new child the adults may represent a haven from the storm and in one school the researcher was entreated with requests to 'hold my hand Auntie' despite her efforts to remain a passive observer. But some children never approach the adult for help and will stand crying alone until someone notices them.

The fact that there are so many children present and so few adults means that minor upsets can easily be overlooked. Fortunate is the new entrant whose own teacher is on duty at the start. In schools with a system of staggered entry the supervisor may know which children are new because they are comparatively few in number. In one school, where children were admitted on their fifth birthday, it was easy for the adult to spot the new individual and be especially aware of his needs.

Three-quarters of the sample children sought out the company of older siblings or friends at playtime and continued to do so throughout the early weeks. Of the rest, a small number appeared to have no problems at all and coped quite happily. Others, however, seemed bored and lonely and remained on the fringe until they had formed peer relationships.

Special arrangements for new entrants

Most infant staff are aware of the potential problems which playtime can cause to newcomers and various strategies are employed by heads and class teachers to mitigate distress. Here are some examples observed:

- Class teacher takes the children on an introductory visit to the play area while everyone else is indoors, explains the system and lets them try out the play equipment.
- Class teacher escorts the children to the play area and remains there throughout playtime in the early days.

- Class teacher points out new entrants to supervisor or introduces them to her.
- Head and reception teachers make themselves available to guide newcomers back to their classrooms and rescue those who are lost.
- New entrants are segregated into a separate enclosed play area for safety and security during the early weeks.
- Younger children are provided with more play equipment including mobile toys.
- A separate area is set aside for more organized ball games. This obviates some of the rough and tumble.
- Younger and older classes have play at different times.
- Each new entrant is paired with an older child who looks after him.

Dinnertime play

This was the playtime which presented the sample children with the greatest discontinuity in their play experience because for most of them it was an entirely new event. The majority had attended their pre-schools for half days only and those who had been in all-day care had not had to cope with this gap between morning and afternoon sessions. Almost all the new entrants stayed to school dinner and therefore had to fill in time between the end of the morning and beginning of the afternoon programmes. This period varied between schools from $1\frac{1}{4}$ to $1\frac{1}{2}$ hours in length. In most of the schools the younger children had their dinner immediately after the close of the morning session, thus leaving a period of 45 to 60 minutes afterwards for play. In one or two schools beginners went to the second sitting, thereby splitting the playtime into two periods of roughly 20 to 30 minutes each. During these dinnertime play periods the children were supervised by ancillary staff, generally known to them as 'dinner ladies', usually the same ones who were in attendance at dinner. These added to the number of adults the new children had to get to know and on the first day one or two beginners plainly missed their teachers.

What do the children DO?

The children are usually expected to play outside except in bad weather when they have to stay indoors. On wet days the new entrants tended to lose track of time, repeatedly asking questions during the afternoon like 'Is it story time?' and 'Is it nearly home time?'

To January starters in particular the long dinner playtime was a source of discomfort and they often showed signs of being cold despite their coats, hoods and mittens. Some tried to slip into the building whenever possible, but this can present supervisory problems and in some schools the classrooms were locked during the dinner break. In one school kindly supervisors allowed chilly youngsters to sit in the cloakroom for a while.

How do children pass the time when they are outside for such long periods? Here are two examples taken from observers' notes; both children are in their third week at school and are not untypical of the sample.

Tracey:

12.30	Damp weather, very windy and cold. Large playground, children aged five to 12.
	Tracey is with older sister and sister's friend, walking about arm-in-arm.
12.40	Holding sister's hand, goes indoors to toilet.
12.50	Stands close to sister looking on at children in playground.
1.05	Goes indoors with sister and disappears into toilet.
	Outside again, sits on a seat, then runs about with sister's friend.
1.15	Alternately leans against wall or follows sister about.
	It starts to rain, children go in early.
1.20	Queues for drawing paper from dinner lady.

Total time: 50 minutes.

Ian:

12.30	Puts on anorak and wanders outside.
12.40	Pushes toy car along wall with another boy.
12.50	Goes indoors to toilet, wanders around in corridor. Red nose.
1.00	Looking at books in corridor with three other children; very chatty.
1.15	Has been running between corridor, classroom and playground with anorak streaming from his head. Not supposed to go into the classroom.
1.25	Goes into classroom and waits in his place.

Total time: 55 minutes.

The striking thing about these and most of the children observed was their low level of activity. Perhaps this was because, in many cases, there was little or nothing for them to play with. Wayne, for instance, was an active child who seemed to have difficulty keeping still and he complained on his first day that 'there's nothing to do'. Three weeks later he was joining enthusiastically in an impromptu game of football on the school field. But for many children ball games were not permissible.

In situations where there is little or no play equipment the child is dependent on himself or other children to invent ways of passing the time. Children with older siblings or friends clung to them from the first and were often included in their play. But those who knew no one were spectators rather than participants until eventually they formed peer relationships. Several of these children, all girls, were engaging in make-believe play with other children by their sixth week.

However, the provision of play equipment is not, by itself, sufficient to keep school beginners happy during the dinner break. At Sundar's school, where new entrants were segregated into a separate playground, there was a plentiful supply of apparatus including slide, square climbing frame with ramps, angled climbing frame, barrels and tyres. Yet this was how Sundar behaved for 30 minutes during his third week:

> Goes off to toilets, returning three or four minutes later. Wanders about or sits around. He seems aimless and alone. Hangs around near researcher. Rolls about on low wall.
>
> Makes no contacts with other children.
>
> Time to line up: has altercation with a girl, they hit each other.
>
> Goes and sits down.
>
> Is called back to line but goes and swings on door handle.

By the sixth week his behaviour was much the same and the observer noted:

> He behaved in characteristically desultory manner, always on the fringe of the group or an onlooker.
>
> He moved around the play area lethargically, sometimes alone, sometimes following other children. Often he stood with eyes half-closed.
>
> He approached other boys verbally several times but never became really involved in any group play. He did not look unhappy but was quick to line up for going indoors.

Contrast this behaviour with afternoon playtime on the same day when he joined older children in the main playground:

> Sundar wanders across playground and climbs on to climbing frame. His manner is desultory.
>
> His special friend, aged seven, comes out to play. Sundar suddenly comes alive. He runs to meet him and they talk and run about together. They are joined by four of his friend's classmates and a chasing game

develops in which the boys periodically fall down 'dead' on the ground. At one stage Sundar organizes the other five boys.

For this child, lethargy and desultoriness were transformed into vitality and obvious enjoyment by the presence of an old friend. No such relationship had been formed with anyone in his peer group during his first six weeks at school, despite being constrained in their company daily for dinnertime play.

How do schools cope?

Heads and teachers are well aware of the potential distress which can be caused to new entrants by the long dinnertime play period. But the large number of children who stay to dinner coupled with limitations on numbers of ancillary staff imposes severe constraints on what they can do about it. Some heads favoured postponement to enable the child to settle in gradually and various strategies were adopted, for example:

- Head urged parents to let new entrants go home to dinner. This met with little success and almost all stayed from the first.
- Children attended school mornings only for the first week and did not stay to dinner until they were attending full-time.
- Children stayed to dinner only after mutual agreement between teacher and parent as to when each child was 'ready'. This arrangement was flexible to allow distressed children to revert to going home to dinner.

Once the new entrants were there for dinner many schools adopted no strategies at all for mitigating distress at play, but the following two examples were observed:

- New entrants were segregated into a smaller play area specially equipped with apparatus for the younger child.
- New entrants had dinner at the second sitting, thus breaking the long play period into two. The first was usually spent watching television in the reception unit. This decreased time in the playground to about 30 minutes.

The disadvantages of segregation from older friends and siblings have already been discussed. On the other hand, the system of a split dinner break seemed to work very well for the sample children observed.

The effect of postponement is difficult to distinguish from other influences. The children who appeared to find playtime least congenial and showed signs of loneliness and boredom were all children who stayed to school dinner from the start but none of them had older siblings or friends present.

Concluding remarks

The concept of compulsory formalized playtime is a new one to most children starting school. What then can be done to take the stress out of the situation? Does the answer lie in the setting, in the system, or in the social relationships?

The physical setting presents the child with a new and wider territory, different or minimal play equipment, and a greater concentration of children than he has hitherto encountered. He is one of the youngest and smallest, and most of the people are strangers to him. The system imposes constraints upon him with signals to obey and routines to memorize. Its compulsory nature may conflict with his natural inclinations, giving rise to boredom and discomfort.

The new child in the playground is typically a bystander rather than a participant and his activity level is low. He sometimes appears lethargic and listless, especially during the longer dinnertime play and may genuinely be tired. He copes with the unfamiliarity of the situation by remaining on the fringe of things or seeking refuge in an adult, old friend or sibling. But at first the adults too are strangers and there are other demands on their attention. By far the greatest solace to the new entrants observed was the presence of brothers and sisters or existing friends. These were sought out not just at first but throughout the early weeks and their absence always had a noticeable effect. They provided the comfort of someone to latch on to in unfamiliar surroundings and afforded a degree of protection and support. Not even a plentiful supply of play equipment could compensate some children for separation from those they knew.

The shortest route to happy playtimes seems to lie in the presence of siblings or existing friends. Where these are not available the child is dependent on the formation of new friendships and these may be slow to develop. The following suggestions are offered for consideration as possible ways of minimizing discontinuities in the newcomer's play experience and of facilitating the development of supportive peer relationships:

- giving new entrants the option of playing indoors or out, especially during the longer dinnertime play

- making the outdoor play area attractive to small children and minimizing discomfort by the provision of sheltered areas, seats and drinking fountains

- creating corners with low walls and seats where children can seek refuge from the tumult of the main play area

- providing play equipment particularly suitable to the younger child's needs, especially portable apparatus and junk during the longer dinnertime play

- making use of parent helpers in the playground during the early days

- pairing newcomers with older children

- breaking up the long dinnertime play with shorter periods before and after the meal or with a variety of indoor and outdoor activity

- above all, wherever possible, giving new entrants the opportunity to play with siblings or established friends.

CHAPTER 10

Staying to Dinner

Staying to dinner at school represents more than a major discontinuity in the experience of young children; for most of them it is a totally new experience. Less than a quarter of the children in our sample of 36 were used to regularly dining away from home. These were the children attending full-time at day nurseries and nursery school or with a minder. The rest usually ate at home. Yet when their parents were interviewed prior to their children starting school, most of them said they wanted them to stay for dinner. Only two said they would prefer their children to come home and four thought they might give it a try. In fact, when the time came, all but one stayed every day.

Hopes and fears

While it is probably easier for a working mother if her child stays to dinner, personal convenience was not given as a reason for wanting their children to have school meals. Instead, parents clearly saw advantages to the child both in remaining at school and in having dinner there. Staying at school would ensure safety and continuity for the child, and save time and energy travelling to and fro. Having a meal there would improve his eating habits: make him less faddy, speed him up, get him used to a wider range of foods. It was a social occasion which would accustom him to eating with others.

However, most parents also had reservations. In response to the general question, 'How do you think X will take to infant school?' nearly half spontaneously expressed worries about dinnertime. These centred around *the situation*:

that the day will seem long,

that he has never eaten away from home before,

that he won't like the noise or the crowds or won't know anyone,

and *the meal*:

that he won't like the food,

that he won't be able to cope with feeding himself or with cutting his meat.

More detailed discussions revealed that these fears were not without justification. Thirteen of the children were described by their parents as poor eaters. Four were slow; nine had poor appetites and were said to be fussy, faddy, finnicky or going through a bad phase.

Only about half the sample children used a knife and fork at home. The rest used a spoon and fork, or fork only. Three children were still sometimes fed by their mothers, either to encourage them to eat more or to save the mess on the carpet. Three more children were attending a day nursery where everything was eaten with plastic spoons, though in all the other nurseries older children were encouraged to use a knife and fork. At least one Indian family traditionally ate with their hands and in a Chinese home knives were not used. In fact it was the knife which seemed to cause most worry. Even the children who were used to a knife and fork at home were said to have difficulty cutting their food, especially meat. Parents assumed that their child would be expected to eat with a knife and fork at school. Competence was of real concern to them and several planned to give their children a crash course on cutlery in the coming weeks.

Head teachers are not unaware of these problems and many of them devise strategies for letting the child start gently. The most common theme is postponement, so that the new entrant does not have to cope with school meals on his very first day at school. There are various ways of organizing this and examples of those observed in our sample schools are given below:

- new entrants attend school full-time from the start but must go home to dinner for the first week or two.
- new entrants attend school half-days only for the first week and may not stay to dinner until they start full-time attendance.
- new entrants attend school half-days only at the start and must go home to dinner for their first full-time week also.
- new entrants attend school half-days only for the first week and may not begin school meals until teacher and parents mutually agree that the child is 'ready'. This arrangement is flexible so that the child can, if necessary, revert to going home to dinner again.

All these strategies were mandatory, thus ensuring that no new entrant could begin school meals until at least his second or third week at school. Three heads, however, adopted the less stringent policy of allowing new entrants to stay from the start, while at the same time strongly recommending parents to let their children go home to dinner in the early weeks. In all cases their advice went unheeded and almost all the children stayed at school.

First meal at school

In view of parents' misgivings about how their youngsters would cope, and heads' counselling that 'it would be desirable for new entrants to go home for lunch during their first term', it is remarkable that so many young children stay to school dinner.

All but one of the 36 sample children stayed and more than half (19 children in five different schools) stayed from their very first day at school. All the others began at the earliest opportunity, with the single exception of a child who missed the beginning of term through illness.

The first school meal is potentially a bewildering experience for the new entrant, a situation to be negotiated beyond the safety of his classroom. There will be rituals and routines, strange faces and places. And, of course, the food. Let us take a look at what lay in store for the children in the study.

Countdown to dinnertime

Graham's introduction to school meals began half-way through the morning when his teacher took him, together with his classmates, on a tour of the school. She was anxious that they should not think the school began and ended with their own room, and the trip concluded with a visit to the school kitchen where they met the cook who told them what was on the menu. This brought forth ecstatic cries of 'Yum, yum!' A similar expedition took place in a second school where the head was concerned that the children should know what lay behind every door and, in particular, should not be scared by a dark alcove in the dining room.

The main preparation for dinner, however, took place after clearing up from the morning's activities. This could take anything from five to 30 minutes depending on the number of procedures involved and the proximity of the facilities. Thus, if the meal was at midday, getting ready for it could make considerable inroads into the morning, especially in the early days. All the preparation routines observed began with toilet and handwashing and ended with walking to the dining area, but there were variations on what happened in between. The personal preferences of individual class teachers might include telling a story or looking at books; methods of organization might involve waiting, queueing, lining up, walking in file; identification of new entrants or children on special diets might entail putting on name tags and coloured bands. In one or two classrooms grace was said, the children standing behind their chairs with hands together and eyes closed reciting a short prayer. Here is an example of what getting ready for dinner was like for Penny:

11.50 going to toilet and washing hands
11.53 looking at a book
12.00 lining up to go into hall.
Time: 10 minutes

Contrast this with Priti's experience:
11.30 lining up at classroom door,
walking in line to toilets,
washing hands,
lining up at washroom door,
walking in line back to classroom
11.50 putting on name tag,
putting on diet band
11.55 lining up at classroom door,
walking to dinner room
12.00 lining up at dinner room door.
Time: 30 minutes

By the sixth week Priti's class were familiar with these procedures and were able to complete them in about 20 minutes, but compared with the ease and simplicity of Penny's routine the pattern was complicated and time-consuming. For Penny and Priti it was their first day at school. For Priti, the mere preparation for her first school meal must have been bewildering. The two routines represent extremes of those observed. By comparing them we can distinguish the factors which influence the development of such different routines and understand why children are subjected to them.

BUILDING DESIGN AND FACILITIES

Penny's was a new school designed so that toilets and handbasins were integrated with the teaching areas. Priti's school was a large pre-war brick building comprising chains of classrooms flanked by long straight corridors. The toilet block was at one end and Priti's classroom at the other, so going to the toilet was a major expedition for the smaller children.

Penny's school was compact, with the hall in the centre and classrooms leading off it. Since dinners were eaten in the hall it was a simple matter for the children to move there from their rooms. For Priti, the dining room was remote and entailed a long walk through the school corridors and across the playground to a terrapin.

A consequence of such dispersed facilities is that children have to be organized and supervised to reach them safely. Priti's teacher was obliged to marshal her pupils along the route, stopping at intervals to allow the slow ones to catch up and periodically reassembling them so that they could all move off together. It was the waiting and assembling as much as getting from place to place which took up so much time. It was not surprising that, at a time of day when energy was ebbing, Priti arrived at the dinner table looking thoroughly dazed.

ADMISSION AND INTAKE

A second group of factors relate to the school's admission system and the nature of the new intake. Penny, in common with the other children at her school, was admitted on her fifth birthday. She was the only new entrant that day and was easily integrated into the system by her more experienced classmates. She was introduced or pointed out to teachers and ancillary staff, so everyone knew she was a beginner and were aware of her needs. Priti, on the other hand, was but one child among four classes of new entrants all of whom started school within a few days of each other. Her classmates were as unaccustomed to the routines as she was herself and consequently slow at mastering them. Everyone had to wait till the last was ready. Priti's teacher had to cope single-handed, helping children with the toilet, drying hands, fastening name tags and distributing diet bands. The need for name tags was a consequence of admitting a large number of new entrants. Tags were worn around the neck and enabled the dinner ladies to identify newcomers. Diet bands were necessary because the school's intake included many children from ethnic groups who adhered to vegetarian or non-pork diets. These boys and girls wore coloured bands to indicate their requirements and would be served accordingly.

Priti was one of the children who had had long experience of eating away from home because she had attended a day nursery. However, meal-times there were a cosy affair with children eating in small family groups with their nursery nurse. At the end of the morning the children were called in from the garden to get ready for dinner. Toilets and handbasins were close to the family rooms where the children ate. When they were ready, the group gathered around the table and chatted or sang rhymes till the trolley arrived with their food. Children observed in another day nursery had more scattered facilities and their routine also included having their hair brushed.

The complexity of pre-dinner routines, then, is largely defined by the design of the building and the number of new children admitted. In most cases there is little that can be done to alter the design. Of the 35 sample children who stayed to dinner 21 were in classrooms with integral toilet and washing facilities, six had facilities outside the unit but nearby, and eight were a long distance from them. With regard to the dining area, ten children had to walk a relatively long way leaving the building and crossing the playground. The rest remained under cover and transferred to the hall, dining room or another classroom. None of the sample children ate in their own rooms at school.

The length of time spent in taking large numbers of young children long distances to get ready and waiting for them to finish could be shortened by having more than one adult available to help them. In some schools welfare assistants or dinner ladies took groups of children to the toilet and helped them wash, and this greatly reduced preparation time. Where more ancillary help is not possible, perhaps there is a case for involving parents with half an hour to spare, or older pupils from a neighbouring school.

The dining area

Our new entrants are ready to go into dinner for their first school meal. Where do they go and what is it like when they get there?

The children observed at dinner attended eleven different schools but only two of these had a dining room which was used almost exclusively for meals. These were described as follows:

- A room in a terrapin in the playground. Cramped and crowded with low ceiling accentuating noise and heat. About 80 children sitting eight or ten to a table. Tables are close together with little space for the adults to move about. Children grouped in classes, all the reception children at one sitting. Vegetarians segregated and identified by green bands. Tables laid with adult-sized cutlery. Busy atmosphere. Several children crying.

- Pleasant room adjoining the hall. Eight tables of eight, mixed ages. Teachers eat at a separate table. The tables are laid with knife, two forks and a spoon for each child; water mugs; salt and pepper. Each table has a number. Plenty of space between tables. Noisy.

Eight schools used the hall for meals. Tables and chairs had to be put out and packed away again and the floor swept afterwards. In some cases the whole area was used, while in others a section was marked off making for a cosier setting. Here are two examples of halls being used as dining rooms:

- Large modern hall with servery to one side. About 150 children at one sitting. About 60 of these bring packed lunches and are segregated at long tables. The rest sit at tables of eight. Staff eat at separate table. Tables laid with knife, fork and spoon. Water available. Very noisy.

- In a recessed part of the hall. Mixed ages. Seven tables of eight laid with knife, fork and spoon; salt and pepper; water jug and beakers. Four dinner ladies supervise and children are exhorted to be quiet throughout.

In one school where the hall doubled as a dining room, the new entrants ate in a classroom (not their own) for the first term or so to give them a calmer atmosphere in a smaller setting:

- Five tables of five, with separate table for packed lunches. Children given a set of cutlery (knife, two forks and a spoon) and each arranged their own. Two dinner ladies supervised, served and assisted them throughout the meal and then took them out to play. Quiet orderly atmosphere.

These examples give an inkling of the kinds of settings, with their attendant degrees of density, noise and bustle, in which our new entrants suddenly find themselves. Not only must they acclimatize to these surroundings; they must also become familiar with the systems which operate within them.

The system

With so many children staying to dinner, schools have had to devise ways of processing large numbers of children through the meals system as expediently as possible. Where numbers are large or space is small several sittings have to be organized. Ancillary staff, usually known to the children as 'dinner ladies',* are required to supervise and minister to needs. Here are two examples of systems observed:

Children file into hall and are directed to places at tables.

Dinner ladies put plates of food in front of each child.

Children start eating straight away.

Dinner ladies remove empty plates and bring dishes of pudding to each child.

Children remain seated until dismissed by an adult.

Contrast this with the second example:

Child joins queue in hall.

On reaching the servery, child selects items from a range of available dishes.

Child takes his meal to a table.

When he has finished, he clears his place and disposes of scraps and utensils.

Child goes out to play.

These examples represent the two ends of a continuum of systems used in the eleven schools. There are striking differences between them in terms of structure, choice and freedom.

In the first, the meal proceeded step by step in distinct stages. The food was ready-served with no choice of content or amount. The children did not move off their seats once during the meal but the adults were continuously on the move serving, assisting, checking and clearing. In fact, the whole procedure was entirely adult directed.

The second school employed a cafeteria system in which the children were treated similarly to members of the public in a self-service restaurant. They queued up, they chose their own food, they selected a seat. Members of the teaching staff did likewise, mingling with the children. Adults were unobtrusive and direction minimal. Yet although the children came and went freely, the ancillary staff quietly monitored the children making sure they ate a reasonable meal and did not throw too much away.

---

* Their official title varies: examples are 'school meals supervisors' and 'dinner controllers'.

In both schools the aim was speed. In the first, dinner was organized into three sittings with a break between each to clean and lay tables. In the second, there was a more continuous turnover with older classes joining the queue later and taking places vacated by the younger ones. Individuals were not pressed to hurry and really slow eaters could take the whole dinner hour if they wanted to.

The other schools in the study employed systems either similar to those exampled or combining features from both. In all cases the aim of expediency was the same but the experience for individual children was very different. This observation of Ian negotiating his way through the dinner system shows the experience of one small child in a big world:

12.00   Bell rings.

Children line up in corridor, boys in one line, girls in the other. They join the queue going into the hall. Ian pushes and shoves. He looks very small. The hall is packed.

12.08   Ian reaches the hatch. His head is barely as high as the counter. He stretches up and is handed a plate of meat pie and salad. He carries it precariously to the table indicated.

Ian grins and chats noisily, wriggling about on his seat. He eats with both hands picking up small bits of salad.

12.10   Dinner lady admonishes him about the way he is sitting and eating. He continues to eat with his hands, picking up big lumps of meat pie. His mates all use cutlery. Ian fools around with tomato between lips. Frequently slumps down in chair with head barely above the table.

Dinner lady comments 'Salad days are not good days.' Ian makes an agonized grimace and stuffs big chunks of meat pie into his mouth. Two dinner ladies bend over him coaxingly. Ian slides under the table but continues chewing.

12.20   Grabs hand of passing dinner lady and grins at her. Fools with children at next table. Picks up fork and stabs at food.

Other children are leaving. Ian lolls and slides on his seat, covering his ears with both hands.

Dinner half eaten.

Dinner lady brings rice pudding. She spoons some into his mouth, his face contorts. He larks about, leaving rice untouched.

He pushes plate towards dinner lady saying 'Yucky, this'. She tells him sharply to eat up. He ignores her.

12.23   Ian is released. He is almost the last. He fetches his anorak and
runs out to play.

Schools staff are sympathetic to the needs of their smallest and youngest
pupils and many of them organize dinner accordingly. Here are examples
of concessions to new entrants observed in different schools:

- eating at first sitting to minimize hunger
- eating at second sitting to break up long playtime
- eating in separate room to avoid the hurly burly of the hall
- sitting near the servery to reduce walking distance
- sitting at lower tables on smaller chairs

In some schools it was possible for children to sit with their older siblings.
Bearing in mind the importance of knowing someone in a crowd of
strangers, some reception teachers accompanied new entrants into the
dining area and a few lingered throughout the meal in the early days. One
boy's face lit up when he recognized one of the dinner ladies as his
neighbour at home.

The food

In view of parents' misgivings about their children's faddiness, it is worth
taking a look at typical meals provided for young children in school. Here
are some examples from the sample:

- pizza, potatoes, crisps, tomato
  custard with jam sauce
- roast beef, Yorkshire pudding, roast potato, cabbage, gravy
  meringue and cream
  milkshake
- meat pie, carrots, peas, mash
  mousse and cream

Similar fare was provided in the day nurseries and nursery school attended
by some of the sample children.

Two schools catered for the dietary requirements of ethnic groups,
providing variations such as:

- luncheon sausage or corned beef or egg and cheese with salad and
  chips

Two schools presented a choice and a typical selection included:

- soup, rolls, crisps
  stewed steak, chicken stew, potato, greens
  jelly, blancmange, doughnut, fresh fruit

Water was available in all the schools, either at the table or from a trolley. Three schools provided salt and pepper on each table and in one or two schools optional extras like mint sauce were served. In four schools the meal always concluded with a piece of apple. Written menus were sometimes displayed, but only one teacher regularly described the forthcoming meal to her pupils, to exclamations of joyful anticipation.

Perhaps the food itself is less important than the way it is presented. Two plums floating in a sea of custard clearly did not appeal to the girl confronted with them, particularly as she had already indicated her dislike of custard. This also suggests that more important than the food is the degree of control the child has over it. She is less likely to finish a meal that is plonked down in front of her than one where she has had some say in what she wants and the size of the serving. Also important is the degree of coercion to finish the meal. None of the sample children were compelled to eat their food; instead they were variously coaxed, urged or encouraged.

The scene is set. Parents have mixed feelings as their children stay to dinner. Schools devise strategies for getting them fed. But how do the children themselves respond?

The child's response

We can examine the child's response with reference to both his observable behaviour and his parents' comments. The researchers observed each child throughout at least two meals at school, one at or near the start and another in his sixth week at school. His parents were interviewed twice: before entry when they were asked how they thought the child would take to school, and again about a month after entry when they were asked how he was settling in. From all this information we can build up a picture of the young child in the school meals situation, noting any sources of difficulty or distress and subsequent progress or regression. Although such information is neither comprehensive nor conclusive, it is nonetheless useful in highlighting problems and seeking ways of mitigating them.

To base judgements wholly on appearances at school would fail to take account of what the child said and did at home. Children who seemed to be coping well sometimes confessed worries to their parents who described them thus: 'He missed his teacher at dinnertime'. 'She couldn't recognize the food or put a name to it.' Almost a third of the parents said their child did not say anything at all about dinner unless prompted, though most parents were concerned to know that their child had eaten, and some also checked with the school. Six parents were pleased with the improvement in their child's appetite since staying at school, though another remarked on the deterioration in her son's table manners. Mostly their comments centred on their children's worries such as food fads and dislike of crowds. Fifteen parents mentioned the importance to their child of having someone there he knew such as a sibling, friend or neighbour.

To the observer there appeared to be three types of response: enjoyment, difficulty and distress.

Enjoyment

Rather less than half the children studied (15 out of 35) seemed to enjoy school meals. These included children who, whenever they were observed, tolerated the situation without any apparent difficulties as well as those who displayed obvious signs of pleasure. But two of these had told their parents they did not like school dinners.

Difficulties

All the other children (20) displayed difficulties of one kind or another. Most of them could be described as poor eaters, picking at their food and eating little. About half had their food cut up for them but only four had real difficulty managing their cutlery. Many children were described by observers as dazed, glazed or bewildered, and stared blankly ahead making little or no social contacts and regarding their food with disinterest. A few burst into tears at times but the cause was not always obvious.

Distress

Six of the children were clearly distressed at school dinners, that is to say they showed signs of extreme discomfort and became upset or depressed. First, a child whose lack of response is disturbing.

Sunil
was an Asian child attending a multiracial school. His mother feared he would not be able to cope with school meals. At home she fed him most of his food and helped him drink his milk. After two weeks at school he

stayed to dinner. His older sister went to a later sitting. A plate of cheese pie, potatoes and beans was put in front of him. His face was expressionless. He did not touch his meal. His teacher cut up his food and urged him to eat. He shook his head. He was told that if he did not eat up he would have to go home. A dish of rhubarb and custard was placed before him and a spoon put in his hand. He put down the spoon and gazed into space. He did not speak at all. When released, he walked slowly outside and stood in the playground looking for his sister. Sunil continued in a similar manner, only eating a little if fed or urged. After a week or so he was absent for four days and on his return refused to eat at all. He sat staring ahead and did not say a word. He was referred to as 'the one who never eats'. That afternoon the head sent home a note to say he would no longer be allowed to stay to dinner.

Next, three children whose distress seemed to centre around the food.

Adam
was a fussy eater who ate only chips, sausages and toast at home. He liked his mother to feed him breakfast in bed with a spoon. At school dinners he sobbed a great deal and ate only when fed. In his fifth week he was looking happier, smiling and talking, but when he was urged to eat up his salad he got upset and began to cry again. At the final observation a week later he still ate little and was fed by four different adults during the course of the meal.

Robin
lived too far from school to come home at midday but could eat at a friend's house if he liked. Robin, however, was eager to stay to school dinners. At his first meal he looked dazed. His teacher coaxed him and fed him with a spoon but he was not interested in the food. Throughout the next two weeks he grizzled or sobbed at every meal. His mother said he got upset when his teacher did not stay. After a holiday, Robin seemed better; he cried briefly, then ate his meal. But by the sixth week, although sociable with his table mates, he appeared to have no interest in the food, resting his head on one hand and refusing when urged.

Tamsin
was expected to be difficult because she was reported to be a poor eater at home. Her mother hoped that staying at school would improve

matters and discussed the problem with the teacher. The teacher was understanding; she stayed in the dining area for a while at the start, alerted the dinner ladies to the difficulty and regularly monitored Tamsin's progress. Tamsin picked at her food and ate little. From time to time she had a few tears. The staff were lenient with her and her mother gave her fruit to supplement the meal. Her teacher asked for a list of Tamsin's likes and dislikes which she passed on to the dinner supervisor. When asked, her mother said she wanted Tamsin to persevere with school meals. She wondered if the noise upset her. By the sixth week Tamsin appeared to be making some progress, seldom crying but rarely finishing a meal.

Now a child whose problems did not centre on the food:

Rosalie
was an only child whose mother feared problems with the school meals situation. The first meal went well and Rosalie looked pleased when she was praised for finishing all her food. Her early weeks were interrupted with school closures and minor ailments, and Rosalie began waking at night with tummy pains which disappeared as soon as she was allowed to stay home. Discussions between mother and teacher followed. Rosalie appeared to be having trouble adapting to the dinner system; she was unused to eating with others and was afraid that without her bib she would spoil her clothes. She worried that she could not always identify the food. Her mother reassured her, gave her a cooked evening meal and told her to do her best. The school staff were lenient and by the sixth week Rosalie was coping with school dinners by eating little and fast to get outside as quickly as possible.

Lastly, a child who could not cope with strangers:

Tracey
had an elder sister in the school and both girls took packed lunches.* Their mother, who went to work, was confident that Tracey, who was described as quiet and rather withdrawn, would be all right with her sister to look after her. At first all was well. Children with packed lunches ate at a long table in the hall which was crowded at dinnertime. Tracey sat next to her sister, eating steadily from her smart new sandwich box. A fortnight later her sister was absent. At dinnertime

---

* Heads are aware that children can be faddy about food and many of them allow children to bring a packed lunch from home.

Tracey went into the hall, hesitated and burst into tears. A dinner lady directed her to a seat but Tracey sobbed and refused to be comforted. Eventually a place was found for her next to an older friend and neighbour from home. Tracey recovered and ate her dinner. She continued to cling to her sister or friend throughout the six weeks. Her mother said Tracey was disillusioned and frightened without her sister, and would be all right if she could come home to dinner.

These six case studies are useful in drawing attention to the difficulties which many children experience but may not manifest so openly. They also underline the importance of three factors which may affect the child's adjustment not only to school dinners but to school in general:
interruptions in attendance
the attitudes of adults
the presence of siblings or friends
Three of the six distressed children had spells of absence in the early weeks. After absence, Rosalie's problems made themselves apparent, Sunil's worsened and Robin's showed only a temporary improvement. In Sunil's case adult attitudes were negative and no attempt was made to help him, whereas Tracey's gradual improvement and Rosalie's survival depended on the patient understanding of parents and staff. The presence of an older sibling or friend was of paramount importance to Tracey, and if Sunil's sister had been with him perhaps he too would have stayed the course.

Progress

Sunil was the only casualty in the sample during the first six weeks at school. We do not know if there were others afterwards. Neither do we know how many improved or regressed later. We can, however, chart progress during the observation period, bearing in mind that the children had been having school dinners for four to six weeks depending on when they began.

no noticeable difficulties	:	15
difficulties overcome	:	2
difficulties persisting	:	17
given up	:	1
Total	:	35

Table of progress observed in children during their first four to six weeks at school dinners.

It is striking that 50 per cent of the sample were still having difficulty after some 20 to 30 school meals. Those with no noticeable difficulties included the two whose parents said their children did not like staying, despite appearances to the contrary, and six who had been reputedly poor eaters at home. The two whose difficulties seemed to be overcome were children who were faddy at home and slow to begin with at school but who nevertheless appeared to cope quite adequately after a while. The children with persisting problems included five of the distressed cases; the sixth was no longer staying. Since so many children were still having problems with school dinners it is worth looking more closely at the nature of their difficulties.

The nature of the problem

Almost all the children displaying difficulties with school meals were observed to be poor eaters, picking at their food and taking a long time over it. Five of these children came from non-European families and were unaccustomed to some of the food and the tools for eating it. In all but two cases poor eating was not unexpected, since these children had displayed similar behaviour at home or in their pre-schools. The other two children, Tracey and Rosalie, were clearly having problems not with the food but with the situation in which they had to eat it. We know that most of the poor eaters had a history of poor eating but we do not know how far their reluctance was exacerbated by the school situation. Certainly there was a connection between the type of meals system employed and the incidence of children manifesting difficulties and distress. Systems in the eleven schools varied in their degree of structure or formality. In the most formal systems the child had minimal freedom of movement and choice of food. He had no control over his meal which was entirely adult-directed. Here is an example:

child is seated from the start
food is put in front of him
the food is ready-served on the plate
utensils are removed
child waits to be dismissed

At the other end of the scale was the informal system in which the child had freedom of movement and choice and played an active part in organizing his own meal:

child joins queue
child chooses food and stipulates amount
child takes his meal to a table
child clears his own utensils
child leaves when finished

The sample schools clustered at each end of the scale, six schools implementing all or most aspects of the formal system and five the informal. The distribution of children responding to these systems with enjoyment, difficulties or distress, may be shown thus:

children's responses	:	number in different systems		
		formal	informal	total
enjoyment	:	3	12	15
difficulties	:	10	4	14
distress	:	5	1	6
	TOTAL	18	17	35

Table showing distribution of children's responses in formal and informal systems.

Most of the children who appeared to enjoy or at least tolerate school meals without problems were in schools employing informal dinner systems, whereas most of the difficulties were observed in formal systems. The single incidence of distress in an informal system was the child who clung to her sister or friend; since she took a packed lunch she was not directly involved in the system and can be discounted. All the other cases of distress occurred in schools which implemented every feature of the formal system. It seems likely, then, that formality and the constraints which go with it may be instrumental in prolonging children's eating problems.

The fact that schools have to process large numbers of children through the meals system as efficiently as possible in a limited time means that there is likely to be a certain amount of pressure to hurry up. If staff are conscious that there are more sittings to follow, they will be tempted to coerce the children to get through their meal quickly. Portions may be set out ready on plates and empty dishes whisked away to be replaced by the second course; children may be repeatedly urged to eat up. These accord with the procedures in more formal systems where there was also a higher incidence of difficulty and distress. Thus formality brings not only procedural constraints but also pressure, and this may be important in prolonging problems. No children were compelled to eat, but slower eaters were repeatedly coaxed, urged or fed, while quicker ones were rewarded with praise or release.

Conclusions

Contrary to expectations, problems were not associated particularly with noise or mass. Instead they were clearly related to formality and pressure. The evidence favours the adoption of a system in which the child has control over his own meal, with minimal constraints on what to eat and how to eat it.

The 'cafeteria' system would seem to best meet these requirements. Each child comes into school with established eating patterns and these can be catered for if he is provided with a range of food items to select from. He can then decide what he wants and how much to have. An argument against this system is that the child may consistently choose an unsuitable diet. This was not the case with the children in the sample. For example, Penny at her first school meal selected crisps, a roast potato and a slice of steamed pudding. But as she grew accustomed to the system her choice became more balanced and by the fourth week she typically selected the following: soup; liver, sausage, potato, cabbage; jelly and biscuit. This was a substantial meal and Penny finished everything but the cabbage. Another advantage of this system is that it removes the need to hurry. Because the meal proceeds on a rolling basis rather than in discrete stages, there is a continuous turnover with later arrivals taking places vacated by those who have finished. Slow eaters can take their time while others come and go.

In view of the great number of young children who stay to dinner and the high incidence of difficulties they experience, there is clearly a need to look carefully at ways of making dinner at school more congenial to new entrants. Distress and difficulties may be minimized or even avoided by taking the following measures:

- ensuring the child is with someone she knows, such as sibling, friend, class teacher

- teaching the child to recognize and name items of food

- providing suitable furniture and a variety of cutlery

- presenting a choice of foods and allowing the child to stipulate the amount

- allowing the child plenty of time

- helping but not coercing

Note

Since this study was carried out, the provision of school meals has been increasingly affected and even jeopardized by rising costs. In some areas schools are offering snack meals or encouraging pupils to bring packed lunches. These changes have implications for the kind of difficulties young children may encounter.

The case studies

The next three chapters are devoted to case studies of individual children starting school. They have been selected from the 36 target children observed in the longitudinal study. They were chosen because their experiences were distinctive enough to highlight critical features of continuity, yet pervasive enough to be of general interest. The descriptions are not meant to be typical of certain kinds of transition; instead, their purpose is to put into perspective some of the issues already discussed, and to illustrate the complex and subtle interplay of influences which affect individual children.

The case studies give detailed pictures of real people; only their names have been changed to preserve confidentiality. The case studies are:

Chapter 11. Ruth and Debbie: twins transferring from a nursery unit to reception classes in another school.

Chapter 12. Graham: a boy transferring from day nursery to infant school.

Chapter 13. Celia: a girl starting school straight from home.

Ruth and Debbie

It is a dark December day and raining steadily as the twins arrive at the nursery unit with their mother and younger sister. Their checked coats are snugly buttoned and hooded against the weather, one blue and one red. Pale-faced and bright-eyed they play around happily outside the nursery where they come daily for the afternoon session. They are early because of the infrequent bus service and must wait till the nursery doors are opened at the appointed time. Their home is five miles away, but their mother, anxious that her children should have a nursery education, feels it is worth the daily journey with scarcely time to get home before returning to fetch them, and apart from a recent bout of whooping cough their attendance has been excellent. 'It's like going to school, it gives them discipline and training', she explains, believing this to be preferable to being with 'other children's mums' in the local playgroup. The twins, just five years old, have been attending the nursery for four terms now, and after Christmas they will be starting school, not here but in their own village. This morning they accompanied their mother and father to their new school to meet their teachers and look around, and this event is still uppermost in their minds as they go into the nursery.

Once inside, they hang up their coats, kiss their mother goodbye and without a backward glance hurry to the story corner. They are warmly clad in similar dresses, one red and one green, and their delicate features are framed in wavy brown hair. Without their hoods it is possible to discern that their apparently identical faces are not quite the same, Ruth being slightly chubbier than her sister Debbie.

In the story corner, backed by a shining collage of gold and silver foil and flanked by bookshelves, the children gather around their teacher for registration. Debbie perches on a bright orange bucket seat, while Ruth sits crosslegged on the rug. As the last of the stragglers drifts in, Debbie is unable to contain herself any longer. 'I went to my new school today', she proclaims proudly. The teacher is responsive: 'How exciting!', and the group listens attentively as Debbie expounds fluently for several minutes. When she pauses for breath Ruth takes up the theme, elaborating and extending her sister's story. Together they paint an enthusiastic picture of the school to which they, the only children from this nursery, will be going.

The nursery

The nursery they are leaving behind is a modern self-contained unit attached to an infant school but standing on its own. It caters for eighty children who attend either the morning or afternoon sessions, 40 in each. It is staffed by two teachers and two nursery nurses. The children are allocated to a group, either 'Reds' or 'Greens', with their own teacher and nursery nurse whom they meet for registration, discussion and stories at the beginning and end of every session. For the rest of the time the groups mingle freely in the single open-plan playroom and the four staff are busily involved in the children's activities.

Preparations for Christmas are well under way and the room sparkles with decorations. Rehearsals take place daily for the Christmas concert in which Ruth is the star of Bethlehem and Debbie a rag doll. There is plenty to interest and stimulate the children during activity time, with Christmas presents to make and a variety of equipment which is set out on tables and changed halfway through the session. Every child's performance is carefully monitored by the staff and they are encouraged to participate in the full range of available activities, from interlocking 'stepping-stones' to catching magnetic fish, from making pastry candle holders to writing their name. They also learn to move expressively to taped radio programmes and to help raise money for relief work in Cambodia.

The twins' favourite is the Wendy House and when they first came they played in there a great deal. Now, although still indulging their love of imaginative and innovative play, they both enjoy puzzles, painting and playing outside. They usually play quite independently, yet their general demeanour is strikingly similar. Both appear eager and receptive to their surroundings. Each works intently at the task in hand, often with feverish intensity. When finished, they look around for something else to do, flitting like butterflies until they find something to settle on. From time to time they pause briefly to yawn or bite their nails before plunging wholeheartedly into the next task. When asked how she thought the twins would like school their teacher replied, 'They will enjoy reading and writing, they are ready to start'.

The home

The twins live in a detached mock Georgian house on a modern estate in pleasantly wooded suburbia. Born prematurely, they weighed just over four pounds each and are not 'identical'. Their sister was born 18 months later. The three girls play together a great deal, re-living visits to the dentist or shoe shop in their imaginative play. Their mother provides them with dressing-up clothes and old blankets, and is happy to let them 'turn the house upside-down' because this is 'how it should be'. She sits with them to watch television using the more questionable programmes as opportunities for discussion. The girls dote on their father who clearly delights in their company, despite his protests that 'house, car and garden are all going to pot'. Their art work has pride of place in the lounge and portrait photographs stand on the window sill. The whole family are thrilled at the prospect of the twins starting school. Both girls want to learn to read and their mother feels 'it would be a sin to hold them back'. Debbie declares 'I'm fed up with nursery school' and her twin explains that 'there's no new work at all, we've done it all'. Their nursery teacher confirms that they 'need to be stretched' and are ready for more directed and structured learning. Their parents are a little apprehensive about the large school playground and the longer school day, but no real problems are envisaged. They want their daughters to go as far as they can, taking the view that 'when you educate a girl you educate a family'.

First day at school

On a cold crisp morning in early January, Ruth and Debbie, snug in their duffel coats, set off to walk the three-quarters of a mile to their new school. At the school gate their mother and little sister pause to greet some other parents and the twins stride purposefully on towards the main entrance. Just inside they are welcomed by the Head, Mr Hargreaves, who bends forward to speak gently to the twins calling them by name. They both answer pleasantly.

A long corridor stretches away before them and the low hum of children's voices comes from behind closed doors. Of the other 200 pupils there is no sign, for this is the second day of term and they have already been busy in their classrooms for twenty minutes or so. Two doors, however, stand open. These are the reception classes, one on each side of the corridor, and one twin will be going into each.

The Head believes that placing twins in separate classes enables them to be seen more readily as individuals. The twins are delighted at the prospect of having their own teachers, Debbie declaring 'Good, I don't want Ruth bothering me'. Their parents also approve, saying they have never really had the chance to know their daughters singly. This will be the first time the twins have been formally parted.

It is to Debbie's classroom that the family goes first. The teacher, Mrs Thompson, stands just inside, and there is a small queue of new entrants and their parents waiting to see her. The older pupils, who have already been at school for a term or two, are busy with their books. When it is Debbie's turn she is greeted quietly and directed to a peg to hang up her coat. On her return, Debbie produces a red exercise book containing drawings and captions done at nursery. Mrs Thompson is young and softly-spoken, and together they look through the book discussing the contents. The teacher gives the impression she has plenty of time for Debbie, and Ruth stands apart looking on. At last, Debbie is told to go and find a seat at one of the tables and her mother moves away saying she will look in again later.

In Ruth's class there is also a queue, so she and her mother go in search of a peg in the nearby cloakroom. Ruth's is identified by her name and a picture of a train underneath. There are nine new entrants in Ruth's class, and each one is given a little yellow badge with their name on to wear. Ruth hands over her nursery exercise book and her teacher Mrs Goodwin puts it on her desk saying she will look at it later. Ruth makes a beeline for a group of children playing a card game on the rug, and is soon too absorbed to notice her mother slip unobtrusively away. Debbie, too, scarcely looks up from her new workbook when her mother calls in to say goodbye. The doctor was right: that headache Debbie had after visiting the school last term was only catarrh and not nerves after all, and Mrs Harris leaves feeling fairly satisfied that her daughters will be all right until she returns this afternoon to collect them.

An hour later the twins are putting their coats on again to go out to play. The whole school uses the playground at the same time and the large rectangle of tarmac is crowded. Ruth's teacher is on duty today supervising the playtime but the twins ignore her. They also ignore each other, striding about the playground with apparent confidence, making frequent verbal contacts with other children most of whom are strangers to them. They separately explore the full range of the play area, but their pink noses suggest they are feeling the cold and they each make repeated trips to the school door as if wanting to go in. Fifteen minutes later the whistle sounds, and the whole school moves towards the door at one end of the building. All except Debbie, who looks lost and starts walking in the opposite direction. She soon realizes where everyone is going, however, and does likewise. Mr Hargreaves stands just inside the door ready to direct anyone who is not sure where to go. Debbie and Ruth both go straight to their respective pegs, hang up their coats, and go into their classrooms.

Their first experience of school dinners passes without incident for the twins. The new entrants are carefully supervised by their teachers throughout the preparatory routines of toileting and handwashing, and are specially catered for in a classroom set aside for their meal, instead of joining the rest of the school in the hall. Two 'dinner ladies' of long experience keep a watchful eye on their charges, explaining and encouraging throughout the meal. The twins do not sit together and appear to enjoy their food in the calm, well-organized environment. The same two ladies supervise them in the school playground during the 40 minutes which ensues between dinner and the afternoon session. Their kindliness extends to quietly allowing new entrants who are cold to sit in a corner of the cloakroom until the bell goes, a concession of which Debbie takes advantage. The twins continue to ignore each other.

The afternoon brings fresh experiences for each of them. Ruth has her first PE lesson on the large apparatus in the hall. She moves with confidence and copes easily with dressing and undressing. However, when she is unable to fasten her shoe buckle quickly, she bursts into tears but Mrs Goodwin soon comes to the rescue.

Debbie, meanwhile, is busy again with her workbook into which she has been copying writing and a picture from a workcard. On completion she is warmly praised by Mrs Thompson who tells her 'Your work is so nice you can show it to the children'. Rather diffidently Debbie takes her book around the class and is soon encouraged by an older boy who exclaims, 'Cor, that's good. You are the best new one!' At the end of the afternoon Debbie is again told to hold up her work to the assembled group who murmur appreciatively. This time Debbie looks pleased.

At three o'clock the twins are chattering happily to their mother as they walk out through the school gate. It is the end of their first day at school.

A week later

One week later Debbie has a minor tummy upset and has to stay home from school for a day. Ruth is reassured by her mother and taken to school by a neighbour. Despite some slight apprehension on her mother's part, Ruth seems to accept the situation and all is well.

The next day, when Debbie returns to school, Ruth shows her first sign that all is not well. She wants her mother to accompany her inside the school to the cloakroom instead of leaving her at the gate as she had begun to do last week. At home she begins waking in the night saying, 'I don't want to go to that new school, I want to go back to nursery school'. Her parents try to reassure her, but at the weekend she refuses to attend Sunday School also. Ruth continues in this manner for about a week, being tearful on arrival at school each morning and having bouts of sobbing in class. Mrs Goodwin is very concerned and comforts Ruth whenever she notices her crying. She is surprised because Ruth had not been at all clinging on her pre-entry visit to the school and had sub-sequently appeared quite happy and confident until now. Ruth's nursery teacher had also expressed the view that Ruth was the more placid and mature of the twins, and would probably cope with school more easily than her sister. Mrs Goodwin concludes that Ruth is missing her twin, but their mother says 'she misses me'. Mrs Harris is glad her daughters are not in the same class since the upset 'could have rubbed off on Debbie too'.

Meanwhile, Debbie exhibits the same behaviour as in the nursery: busy, lively and sociable. Her teacher is pleased with Debbie's progress and frequently praises her work. Debbie has a news book in which she copies sentences and draws pictures. She has her own simple reading book and a sentence-making folder into which she inserts all the words she can recognize. Among the art work on the classroom walls are Debbie's collage of a clown and another of shapes cut out of wallpaper. Last week the class led assembly, and Debbie astounded her teacher by holding up a picture and reciting a sentence before the whole school. Debbie seems unaffected by her twin's behaviour. Yet Mrs Harris remembers the time when Ruth had been absent once from nursery school and it was Debbie who cried every day for a fortnight afterwards. It was Debbie too, who was described by the nursery staff as 'the more nervous twin', becoming so agitated when the hosepipe flew off the tap one day in the nursery kitchen that her father could not use his garden hose for months afterwards. He also recalled the day at home when a cardboard box left on the cooker had burst into flames. It was Debbie then who was terrified by the incident whereas her sister was apparently unaffected. Now, after one week at school, the twins' behaviour is the reverse of that which might have been expected.

Playtime seems to have become another difficult time for Ruth. She bursts into tears in the playground and is comforted by Debbie who puts a protective arm around her or holds her hand. The twins no longer stride confidently about but together hang around the member of staff on duty. Their teachers have noticed that the twins 'play together all the time' now. Once back in her classroom Ruth temporarily recovers her composure. After dinner, Debbie waits for her sister and they go out to play hand in hand. They remain close to the supervisor, either holding her hands and chatting to her or clinging to each other. Despite their hooded coats and mittens they find the winter playground a chilly place and after a while they slip into the cloakroom to warm themselves. Ruth complains to her mother that 'there's too much playtime'.

Six weeks on

The twins have been at school for six weeks now and we can look back at some of the behaviours which seem to have become characteristic of them over the last month or so.

In the playground

Playtime continues to cause Ruth some distress though her twin never complains. Debbie seems to have adopted the role of protector towards her sister and the twins are rarely seen apart in the playground. Almost always they walk about as if glued together, Debbie's arm around Ruth's shoulder and Ruth's arm around her twin's waist. At first, both girls had been friendly towards other children, making approaches and initiating contacts. Ruth, however, was rebuffed several times by older children and became quite upset. Her mother explained to her that there are 'all kinds in the world' and advised her to 'stick to children of her own age.' Ruth's confidence has been shaken by the incidents and now she makes only occasional brief overtures to other children in the playground. Debbie, on the other hand, tends to make more contacts but when her sister was absent she spent much of the playtime wandering alone. The twins seem to find the dinner playtime long and often stand around near the school door, slipping inside from time to time. When the whistle sounds they are among the first to go indoors, wasting no time in removing their coats and going into their respective classrooms.

In the classroom

Ruth has got over her tearful stage and both twins leave their mother at the school gate in the mornings, coming together into the corridor with their satchels on their backs. Only once has Debbie burst into tears, sobbing to her teacher that she had forgotten to kiss her mother goodbye, but she was soon comforted and reassured. In both classes the twins are with children who have been at school one or two terms, as well as with other beginners. Ruth's classroom, however, contains more activities for the younger children such as a shop, Wendy House and sandtray, all of which are popular with Ruth. Debbie's classroom is in a modern extension to the old building and incorporates toilets and coatpegs, whereas Ruth's cloakroom is a short distance up the corridor and the toilets are in a separate block connected to the main building by a covered way.

Ruth's class is organized according to age into groups called 'tigers', 'elephants' and 'monkeys' by which children are allocated to activities and PE teams. They are expected to complete set tasks in literacy and numeracy during the morning before moving on to art, craft and a wide choice of other activities in the afternoon. Mrs Goodwin moves around the room closely monitoring what the children are doing, directing and assisting them. She is very busy. New entrants are not given formal work at the start but are encouraged to explore the activities first, being weaned on to the more formal tasks when they are ready. Mrs Goodwin says she does not believe in 'pushing the children but prefers to let it come.'

In Debbie's class the children are expected to work through a number of set activities during the day. These include numeracy, literacy and an art or craft activity. Each activity is carried out at a specific table and the children may choose in which order they do them. They aim to complete all their tasks by the end of the day and those who finish earlier may choose from a large number of other activities which have been set out by the teacher. Mrs Thompson seats herself on a chair in the middle of the room and children come to her for their work to be checked. She dislikes queues, so the children rarely have to wait long for her attention. She is generous with her praise and children who have done well are asked to show their work to the class who join in her acclaim. Similarly, the class is encouraged to reinforce their teacher's disapproval of any poor work or bad behaviour.

Debbie seems to thrive in this environment and is soon able to complete all her set tasks with time to spare. She attacks each activity with such fervour and speed that she sometimes gets careless and is told to try again. By dinnertime she usually looks pale and tired but manages to be attentive and contributory during formal sessions. Neither she nor her sister tolerates inactivity and each of them retains the tendency to flit about the room looking for something else to do.

Ruth, too, tackles each task with intensity and can sometimes be seen hurrying about the room with a worried frown on her face. From time to time she rubs her hand across her brow and her teacher exhorts her to 'Smile!' When she is waiting for Mrs Goodwin's attention she is restless and paces up and down with impatience. She is very precise, tidying and straightening the apparatus in the room. She often works without reference to the children around her and seems happy to play alone. Debbie, on the other hand, is quite chatty with her classmates and seems to get on well with the older ones. Both girls are politely spoken, saying 'Please' and 'Excuse me' to their companions.

Debbie has been encouraged to copy words and pictures from the start and now has several exercise books in which she works. She has a tin in which to keep all the words she can recognize and a reading book which she takes home every evening.

Ruth is described by her teacher as 'a bright little girl' who is 'getting on well with her word-building and counting'. She is very proud of her new sentence-making folder and has recently started on the reading scheme. She is not yet allowed to take her book home.

At home

Mrs Harris is pleased that her daughters come out of school happy, particularly Ruth who she says 'needs a lot of encouragement'. She finds herself trying to listen to both twins at once, and when they get home

Ruth sometimes stamps off upstairs shouting, 'You don't understand'. Ruth finds the school day a long one and arrives home tired, though she soon recovers. The twins play 'schools' a great deal, and writing and colouring are favourite pastimes. When their father comes in they both read aloud to him from Debbie's school book.

Mr and Mrs Harris are pleased that Debbie brings her book home and would be happy for both twins to do homework. They feel that Debbie is being 'pushed to the limits' and this suits her temperament. Mrs Harris has already taken up an informal invitation to call in and see Debbie's school work and is amazed at what her daughter can do. She wonders whether the same environment would have presented Ruth with more of a challenge or whether she responds best to her own teacher's 'gentler approach'. She will reserve judgement until she attends a parents' evening after halfterm.

DISCUSSION

This case study serves to highlight the stress and distress a child may experience after starting school even when the prognoses are favourable. The twins had attended a nursery unit for four terms so a school atmosphere was not entirely foreign to them. The adults with whom they came into contact both before and after transition – parents, teachers and school head – were all caring and concerned for the twins' welfare. The infant school staff each had well-thought-out philosophies upon which they based their provision for new entrants. Yet despite all these, one of the twins, Ruth, displayed signs of distress after one week at school and continued to do so for the rest of the observation period.

There appear to be two possible sources of Ruth's distress: separation from her twin and the school playground. Yet neither of these presented any apparent problems at the beginning. It was as if a trigger was required and that trigger was the one day's absence of her twin. Even then, symptoms did not appear until her twin returned to school the next day. It would be interesting to speculate whether Ruth would have had any problems had her sister not been absent, or whether the reverse would have been the case if Ruth had been absent instead. All we can do is note that when Ruth had been absent in the early days of nursery school it was her sister who had become upset afterwards, but when Ruth was again absent for one day in her fourth week in the infant school neither she nor Debbie was affected. We must also bear in mind that our interpretations can be based only on those signs and symptoms which were observable, and on comments made by teachers and parents.

Separation from twin

The question of how far Ruth's distress could be attributed to separation from her twin is a complex one. The indications at nursery were that the girls wanted to be independent of each other. They usually played separately in the unit and rarely sat together in formal group sessions. There they shared the same teacher and nursery nurse, and were looking forward to having separate teachers at school. But independence need not preclude interdependence. Perhaps the shared nursery environment allowed them the personal freedom they each desired together with the knowledge that their sister was never far away.

The infant school head's reasons for separating the twins were firstly that they could develop as individuals and secondly that one twin should not predominate over the other. Certainly the twins, who appeared so similar in their ways when observed in the nursery, began to display more individual behaviour in their infant classrooms. On the other hand, the precedence of one over the other became apparent in the playground where Debbie seemed to emerge as protector of her more vulnerable twin. We do not know how much the emergent individuality was due to differences in temperament, since their mother remarked that the 'long day', the 'lots of playtime' and rebuffs from older children of which Ruth complained seemed to have no deleterious effect on Debbie. What we can examine, however, are the disparate environmental influences brought to bear upon the twins by assigning them to different classes.

CLASSROOM ORGANIZATION

Both reception classes consisted of children who ranged in age from just five to nearly six and who were in their first, second or third term at school. In Debbie's class the emphasis was on 'work', the word used by teacher and pupils to define tasks which consisted mainly in writing things down such as news, sentences, stories and computation. The children had several different exercise books in which to 'work'. There was a great variety of activities and equipment – much of it made by the teacher – to stimulate them. They were generously praised for 'good work' and individuals were encouraged to seek further approval from their peers. The orientation was towards striving for success.

In Ruth's class the new entrants were at first allowed to 'play', defined as exploring the activities, and there was a range of equipment provided with the younger children in mind. The teacher adopted a child-centred philosophy allowing each to develop at their own pace.

There were three observable consequences of the different teacher approaches: the organization of tasks, the availability of the teacher's attention, and the allocation of homework.

THE ORGANIZATION OF TASKS

In Debbie's class, tasks were allocated on a daily basis. Tasks included literacy, numeracy, art and craft, and if the child completed his quota for the day he was rewarded with free choice from a limited range of attractively presented alternatives. This method allowed the child the flexibility of deciding in which order to do the tasks while at the same time giving him the stimulus of having to complete a number of different activities. Ruth's day was more segmented with literacy and numeracy being completed first, usually in the morning, before going on to an art and craft activity and choice. Children were directed to each specific task by the teacher.

AVAILABILITY OF TEACHER'S ATTENTION

Ruth's teacher rarely sat down at her table except to hear children read to her. Most of the time she was seen moving around the classroom closely monitoring what each child was doing. With 22 children in the class this kept her busy and because her pupils worked at individual stages, she was talking almost continuously. Yet although the teacher was working ceaselessly, any one child could claim only very small part of her attention for himself. For Ruth, who found waiting intolerable, this was a source of frustration. She sometimes required short but frequent spells of attention from Mrs Goodwin in order to carry out a task and displayed impatience when she could not get it immediately. Sometimes she left her chair and paced up and down with a perplexed frown on her face. On occasions the promised help was delayed because the teacher was diverted by another child on the way.

There were the same number of children in Debbie's class but the system of allocating tasks for the day made for flexibility and a more relaxed atmosphere. Mrs Thompson seated herself in the middle of the room and the children went to her. She disliked queues but there were rarely more than two or three children waiting at one time, probably because there were always some at the art and craft activity and they required less of her attention. By assigning activities to specific tables the teacher could, if necessary, go to a table and give attention to the whole group there. This was especially useful for the children at the painting table. When Debbie was trying to complete a partitioning exercise in her number book, she was able to go to her teacher five times in three minutes and during these short exchanges learnt step-by-step what to do.

It is possible that Ruth may have needed more adult attention than her sister since her mother attributed some of Ruth's distress to the fact that she was missing her. Neither she nor the school head attributed Ruth's tears directly to separation from her twin.

ALLOCATION OF HOMEWORK

From her first day in school Debbie had been encouraged to work hard and strive for success. It was not surprising that her eagerness to take a task home each evening was also encouraged. This usually took the form of reading some pages from her school reading book or learning the relevant words to put in her word tin. Ruth, on the other hand, was not permitted to take a reading book home during the weeks she was observed but nevertheless wanted to copy her sister. Ruth's tantrums at home may have stemmed from tiredness. But by not having her own 'homework' to do she was unable, probably for the first time in her life, to strive equally with her twin for the approval of her parents. Sibling rivalry could have been another contributory factor to Ruth's unease.

The school playground

The marked change in the twins' behaviour after the first week could be attributed to several possible causes. The playground was the only place where they could be together, because although they shared the same room for dinner and assembly their appointed places were some distance apart. Their initial blatant avoidance of each other changed to equally blatant physical contact. In the playground the twins became as one, making only occasional brief sorties away from each other. Ruth was the one who was distressed and Debbie was her protector. This distinction between protector and protected was reinforced by the rebuffs Ruth received from friendly approaches to older children in the playground. Both girls were of a sociable disposition towards other children, but whereas they had been among the oldest in the nursery unit, this was the first time they had come into regular contact with children up to eight years old. Three times a day, at appointed times, they were constrained to play outside in the company of about two hundred children of whom they were among the youngest. They often sought the proximity of the supervising adult who probably represented some kind of refuge from the hurly burly.

The twins found playtimes, particularly at dinnertime, long and cold. The playground was a large rectangle of tarmac devoid of play equipment. How to pass the time in such surroundings especially in cold winter weather seemed to present the twins with a problem, especially when they found other children unapproachable.

This was a school where head and staff treated new entrants with special care and consideration. They were aware of the twins' discomfort in the playground but felt they had done all they could. New entrants were encouraged to go home to dinner, and those who stayed at school were given their own room to eat in with two supervisors who also accompanied them outside. The head was constrained by shortage of further ancillary help to do more.

Concluding remarks

The discussion on Ruth's distress has centred mainly around classroom organization and the school playground. With regard to the classroom, the success of any teacher's approach must depend in part on the individual pupil. What suits one child does not necessarily suit another. Debbie appeared to thrive on the stimulus and challenge of her class environment but we do not know whether Ruth would have flourished had she been in the same class or indeed how each twin might have fared had they exchanged classes. The importance of interaction between a child and his environment and between a child and other people in that environment must not be underestimated.

The playground, too, is a setting in which survival very much depends on the individual. However, distress associated with physical factors such as the size, shape and nature of the play area and with organizational factors such as numbers and age range of the children and length and frequency of playtimes can be mitigated in various ways. Similarly, there are a number of possible strategies for coping with the child's personal need for stimulus or attention.

CHAPTER 12

Graham

The child

It's his eyes you notice first. They are large, brown, heavily-lashed, rather slanted, liquid eyes that made a definite impression on several professionals involved with the child: day nursery staff, teachers, the paediatrician and researchers. As his teacher commented on their first meeting 'He came with those big, wide eyes, very strange sort of wild look in his eyes', 'only part that moved were the big eyes that flickered everywhere'.

Physically Graham's a strong, tall, sturdily-built child who looks healthy and well cared for. His brown, very shiny hair flops engagingly over his face and his fair, translucent skin positively glows. A first impression seems to fit with the comments of his day nursery nurse: 'He's lovely isn't he? One of my favourites. He's usually the first in the morning and he's lovely company, very entertaining . . . he'll share a joke. I took to him straight away. He's really super'.

However further investigation shows this boy in a rather different light as he nears the end of his time in a local authority day nursery and looks ahead to his entry to 'big' school after Christmas. Reports from the paediatrician, the social worker's recommendations, the matron's detailing of Graham's improvement and, perhaps most importantly, Graham's behaviour and responses present a coherent picture of the influences which have been at work before Graham walks through the school door in January.

Home and the early years

Graham's was a difficult birth, a breech delivery with birth asphyxia. He joined a family consisting of father who worked as a postman in a psychiatric hospital and mother who was a full-time housewife looking after Julie, a daughter of 17 months. The mother's domestic responsibilities were interrupted occasionally by admissions to the hospital where her husband worked, as she suffered bouts of severe depression. Graham failed to thrive in the early weeks of life and showed some developmental delay. He was hospitalized as a baby and has attended Murryfield hospital every year since for assessment. Certainly the parents remember Graham's early life as traumatic '. . . spent the first three months in hospital . . . had severe croup when one year old . . . always had conjunctivitis . . . nearly lost him . . . had to give him special foods'. The mother suggested that the difficult birth had 'something to do with the problems we still have', even though the doctor had maintained that the damage was rectified.

Graham's home is a clean, tidy comfortable council house in a pleasant cul-de-sac. At the time of the first parent interview the living room was decorated for Christmas with a tree, and a very large mound of presents filled a corner. The matron of the day nursery made the point that sometimes Graham is 'different on a Monday when he's been at home and he gradually unwinds during the week'. The tension he's unwinding from is apparent when visiting the home. The atmosphere appeared emotionally charged largely due to the mother, who spoke sharply to her husband, ordering him to make tea, while she lay motionless along the sofa. For his part the father remained calm and patient, seeming embarrassed by her manner. When either of the children raised their voices, as they did frequently, the mother screeched at them to 'be quiet!', while father suggested quietly that there was no need to shout.

Mother and father seemed to have little idea of what could reasonably be expected of children at various developmental stages. However, whereas father seemed confused and amenable, mother's inadequate knowledge seemed to be combined with a profound lack of sensitivity to her children and their needs. Graham's mother herself had serious problems and while the history of these is not known her actual behaviour can be documented. Without attempting to judge such behaviour, it is possible to record conversations, all occurring within hearing of both children, that indicate deviations from conventional mother–child relationships.

The following are examples:

i) Mother stated that normally Graham was bad with strangers and that on meeting his new teacher he'd been extremely upset –

detailed description of how Graham had behaved on his pre-school visit, appeared to have regressed severely and clung to mother. Mother used whiney sarcastic tone throughout this story and laughed viciously when she described his fear. At this point Graham left the room, his face contorted with distress.

ii) Graham was described in derogatory terms by his mother, insults punctuated by her expressions of a desire to 'wring his neck' for much of the time. Father tried to counter such statements.

iii) Very scathing account of how Graham had gone out onto the nearby major road on his bicycle and had been apprehended by neighbours who'd brought him back whereupon he'd stated firmly his intention to leave home. Mother and sister both joined in a 'good laugh' about the incident while father shuffled uncomfortably in his seat.

It is difficult to assess environments and to form conclusions about what is 'good', 'bad' or 'healthy' and inevitably some intuition creeps in. However, by almost any reasonable standard elements of Graham's homelife seem likely to retard or distort his intellectual, social and emotional growth. The recognition of a home that could be deleterious to the child's development prompted the paediatrician to recommend, when Graham was 22 months old, that a day nursery place be made available.

Pre-school experience

It was just two days after his second birthday that Graham was admitted to the day nursery, a transition that he made at some cost. According to his parents Graham took 18 months to settle, though the matron had estimated it to be 'several' months before Graham settled to the nursery's routine. In this early period he was unable to express his feelings, to respond to others or to make use of the materials. Graham was seen to have 'no idea of how to play' and as being 'unreceptive in every way'.

Graham spent a considerable amount of his waking time in the day nursery, being the first to arrive in the morning at about 7.45 and one of the last to leave. The boy, usually rather reluctant to leave the building at 5.20 p.m. or so at the time of this study, is a striking contrast to the new entrant who had been described as 'shy, awkward and contrary, difficult for us to cope with at all'. Reports from the nursery staff maintained that they had seen a 'remarkable' change in the child in that after his period of adjustment he'd developed into a lively, happy little boy with a distinctive sense of fun. His vocabulary had grown daily and his periods of frustration diminished.

Despite Graham's initial trauma the indications are that his nursery days were extremely important in facilitating his development. Perhaps most importantly the day nursery provided compensatory adult-child relationships enabling Graham to relate to staff in a way that could reap great rewards in the future. In a sense Graham was 'set apart' from his peers by the intensity of his relationships with staff and by his sustained periods of concentrated activity. The day nursery provided Graham with new experiences and activities, encouraging him to develop fine motor skills and hand-eye coordination. Favourite activities, for Graham, were jigsaws and 'cutting and sticking'.

Graham's mother commented, 'I couldn't cope at all and they (day nursery staff) did the job for me'. She suggested that the day nursery had provided a 'home from home' and while one takes her point, the comparison is debatable. The nursery staff provided an environment where not only was Graham provided with experiences, but he was accepted and cared for in the fullest sense. Credit seems due to the staff involved in that, according to nursery reports, Graham 'can achieve almost all that a normal $4\frac{3}{4}$-year-old will do, rarely lagging behind his friends. He can competently and confidently use social skills, knows all shapes, colours etc. and asks for and retains information'.

Clearly there were positive gains and while warm adult bonds were formed, no clear policy was directed towards Graham and he lost developmentally by the constraints of the institution. The length of the day was accentuated by the physical setting in that the children spent their time in one room in extremely cramped conditions. A large, pleasant outside play area was available, but this was only occasionally used outside the summer months. There was a great deal of aggressive behaviour, fighting and disruption in the room – often bordering on chaos. Many of the 18 or so children in the room daily showed evidence of emotional disturbance and reports suggested that every child came from a 'problem' home. Graham's lack of interest in retaliation and aggressive play probably contributed to his forming relationships with staff. Graham had little interaction with his peers, seeming to gain most satisfaction from completing tasks (usually self-selected) and receiving adult praise – on receipt of which he visibly glowed.

The day nursery had helped Graham to catch up, most noticeably in his emotional development. However the nursery had limitations and ceased to be challenging, giving Graham little opportunity to develop further linguistically or socially. Staff attempts to help were thwarted by the realities of the environment – there was a pronounced element of 'batch-processing' and the demands of the other children, most of whom were significantly younger than Graham, were considerable. How would Graham fare at school? Both parents and nursery staff reported how distressed Graham had been since his pre-school visit. The mother was 'expecting anything' and the nursery staff felt that 'he'd be all right except that he'd go into his shell at first', as he had done when experiencing change in the day nursery. How Graham himself felt we do not know, except that after his school visit he did not want to go back to the day nursery, he wanted to go to school. There are various interpretations one could make, but given the available evidence it seems reasonable to suggest that Graham felt that if this much valued source of support and care was going to reject him, he had better do the rejecting first.

School entry

The scene is set – Graham's first day at school. The teacher's expectations have been shaped by Graham's behaviour on his pre-school visit and she's curious due to the mother's comments about her son who 'can't do anything, is a baby'. What of Graham's feelings? He knew school was 'grown-up', his sister went there and he knew that you wore a uniform and that someone called Mrs Whitehead was there. His mother had prepared him by saying that 'he'd better stop wetting his bed' and had 'better learn to write his name' now that he was going to school. Two days previously mother had been admitted to psychiatric hospital suffering from depression and so it was his father who brought Graham to school that day, Graham being the first child to arrive.

An empty classroom, looks very stark. Mrs Whitehead had been laying out tabletop toys to 'greet the new ones'. Graham looks fairly relaxed, father rather nervous. Mrs Whitehead greets Graham warmly and says that she's had a talk with Julie and knows what he's had for Christmas. Graham responds to this – an outburst with a smile 'I had lots of cards'. Mrs Whitehead 'oohs' and 'aahs' and says that she's excited as she's got to find out about Christmas and birthday (Graham was five yesterday). Considerable effort made to welcome Graham. Rest of class enter gradually, Graham settled with Meccano. Father leaves after a few minutes – no response from Graham. Register read out, all children respond on their names. When Graham's turn comes teacher says, 'Can you say "Yes Mrs Whitehead".' Graham nods his head, but doesn't say it. A girl says, 'aah, he's shy'. Mrs Whitehead is patient and explains that Graham can practise saying it by himself.

So it begins. The consensus of opinion among the adults concerned with Graham was that he'd find it difficult starting school and he clearly did. The paediatrician had described Graham in her last report (a month earlier) as 'basically a very able boy who will do well at school. I think he will take time to settle down and will be very unresponsive at first'. That this was so can be illustrated, though only time could tell whether the paediatrician's recommendation that 'he should not be underestimated' would be substantiated.

Graham 'made his mark' right from the start. Within 20 minutes of being in school, Mrs Whitehead called the new children (12 new entrants) to come and play a game, i.e. pick up the badge with their name on. All the new children jumped up enthusiastically and went to the desk except for Graham. Mrs Whitehead took the badge over to him and he made no response. Graham seemed very much the outsider, standing stiffly, arms out at the side, giving other children the odd sideways stare. That first day established a pattern as Graham moved as if in a trance, never responding appropriately to the overtures made to him.

Behaviour in school

Graham was clearly a source of concern to his teacher. Despite having a class of 30, she had given considerable thought to his behaviour and had clear ideas about strategies to be used. Graham's unusual ways did not go unnoticed and the teacher was very concerned that he should not in any way be labelled. Two weeks into term the teacher enthused about Graham – 'I think he's a darling. I've a very soft spot for him,' adding though that it was very difficult to get him to participate.

School represented a dramatic change for Graham in that there were now certain expectations held of him as he confronted new and challenging experiences. Now he was mixing with children of his own age in a more controlled environment where his behaviour was, to some extent, monitored. Changes were expected. To his teacher Graham's unacceptable behaviour was a challenge to which she responded with patience and skill, finding her reward in his success. Graham's tendency to squeak when thwarted was consistently negatively reinforced – such utterances being either ignored or frowned upon depending on their context. Mrs Whitehead spoke warmly of the time four weeks into term when Graham had walked through a group of seated children with an 'excuse me' rather than the customary shrill squeak. Graham's difficulty with communication, often characterized by bouts of echolalia (senseless repetition), received attention and was meeting with some success.

The number of one-to-one sessions with Graham were obviously limited by the other demands made upon the teacher, but the atmosphere of warm acceptance provided a more diffuse positive reinforcement. When Graham had been in school for six weeks his teacher reported that she had seen develop in him 'a general happiness and relaxation that was lovely' and that he made significant strides in a short space of time.

Graham was being allowed to unfold and develop at his own pace, but not in the *laissez faire* way this might suggest. Rather he was provided with a very responsive learning environment that protected him from negative experiences e.g. being singled out in group activities as being the only child not participating, and yet which acted upon his initiations, positively responding to and building upon them. Perhaps a report of a specific incident will help to illustrate the way in which Graham was being handled.

Fourth week of term, Graham has never participated in any music and movement sessions. Children enter the hall and a record is put on. Graham, as usual, slides about and wiggles when he's supposed to be sitting silently listening. The music stops – children asked what it reminds them of – several say soldiers. Children directed by teacher to march as soldiers to the music. Graham marches, he circles the room with stiff movements, arms held out at his sides. (At this point the teacher reports that she's done this session deliberately as she feels soldiers have caught Graham's imagination. Yesterday he had saluted her at playtime and had marched off after the class had been discussing soldiers.) The children continued to march, then paired and marched in columns – first time Graham has been involved in the group instead of just standing on the sidelines.

A similar incident occurred in a PE session the following week when despite the fact that he was visibly trembling from head to toe, Graham climbed a slanted form and negotiated the wall-bars to get down (the latter with teacher's assistance). Graham was praised lavishly for this and he positively skipped onto his next task – the balancing bar.

Graham seemed to thrive on some of the new experiences available, notably imaginative play. He would, on rare occasions, enter the Wendy House where he would play alongside rather than with the other children. His rather immature, unwieldly, loud form of imaginative play did not inspire other children to include him in the game in progress. Graham seemed to be in his element when, with a tea towel wrapped around his waist, he would be Wonder Woman or some such character steering a spaceship through the stars. Graham had a chance to be himself, to enjoy himself and to find expression for his thoughts. One day he decided, at lunchtime, that he was the teacher now and this he announced publicly. He gave his orders, eyes shining and face aglow, to the class – 'stand behind your chairs', 'eyes closed', 'stand quietly Phil'. He was politely and deliberately ignored by the teacher all bar a slight controlled smile that puckered the corners of her mouth.

Conclusion

Graham's first experiences were with a mother who both encountered and created problems in child care. The paediatrician described Graham's family as consisting of 'an intolerant loud-mouthed mother, a jealous older sister and a peripheral father'. These phrases are value-laden, but what does seem clear is that Graham's early development was stunted. He was in a situation where his shortcomings and attempts to learn were scorned. In the day nursery he was enabled to progress in a setting that supported and accepted him and where he grew to be a valued member of the institution. Indeed the reputation Graham had built for himself proved valuable as there was communication between the staff in both school and nursery that alerted the former to the fact that the latter had confidence in the child. Clearly Graham was a 'difficult' child and Mrs Whitehead in particular, was strengthened in her resolve to cope upon hearing that other people felt this way.

The teacher's policy of being kind, but firm and of responding to Graham's 'hunger for affection' undoubtedly helped him to relate to the new world he was exposed to. Graham will be in Mrs Whitehead's class for only two terms before he moves on, receiving another jolt to his seemingly rather fragile internal security. He struggles with new situations and is thwarted by adults who in his teacher's words 'don't know the approach'. The extracts described fall short of capturing the emotional quality of some of Graham's experiences, though the actual words spoken about the child have been used where they describe more eloquently that quality.

Graham's mother appears surprised and gratified by Graham's behaviour since he started school and feels that he should have started in this class when he was four and a half. This represents quite a change in stance for someone who felt Graham would never cope with ordinary school, but that he was 'ESN material'. What of Graham himself? When asked in general terms how Graham liked school his mother pointed to the child who was strutting around the living room head rocking, face aglow singing, albeit rather tunelessly, she replied, 'well, just look at him now, he never used to sing, we never heard it before'.

CHAPTER 13

Celia

Home background

Celia's parents live in the same detached bungalow they had first moved to when they married 13 years ago. It's in a pleasant, spacious close and has a good sized rear garden and a front lawn providing safe outdoor play space. The mother commented that 'sometimes we get so that we want to move', possibly to shorten her husband's daily journey to work in a large town some 25 miles away. However, the family seems well established in the area and they 'wouldn't want to take the children away from school'. 'The children' refers to Don, a boy of eight, Mary, who is ten, and Celia who, when this study began, was approaching her fifth birthday.

The father works as a draughtsman and, due to his commuting, does not arrive home until 7.0 p.m. The family income is supplemented by his working locally all day Sunday so the time spent together as a family is limited. The mother had given up full-time employment before the children had been born and had no plans to return to work. It would seem fair to describe the family as child-centred in that neither parent had interests outside the home and financial resources for luxuries were spent on the children as evidenced by, for example, the large rocking horse, electronic TV game, guitar and large supply of games in the home.

From conversations with the mother it appeared that family occasions, such as Christmas, were eagerly looked forward to by all family members. On one occasion father was expected home early for a birthday tea in Celia's honour and he always took time off to attend the school functions and to accompany each child on their pre-school visit.

Celia's relations with her siblings were said to be 'very friendly though, of course, they fight sometimes'. The two elder children were said to be doing well in school, though they had had some behaviour difficulties with Don that seemed to be subsiding. Mary had attended a playgroup for a year before school and hadn't particularly enjoyed it. Don had 'gone hysterical' at the idea of going and presumably the fact that he had taken to school 'beautifully' had added weight to the mother's feeling that Celia had nothing to gain from attending. Celia belonged to that group of children who, because of their diminishing numbers, were found to be so difficult to locate in this study – children who do not attend any pre-school.

For these home children there may be no suitable places available or, as was the case with Celia, parents may choose not to take up the opportunities in the area. Both older children had started school with the same reception teacher, who had since retired, and the teacher Celia was to go to had taught Don in the top infants class. Celia had been on a pre-school visit to her school and had thoroughly enjoyed it. She told her mother that she needn't stay and had played happily with a little boy. From the evidence of discussions with the family and observations carried out in the home it would be difficult to imagine a child better prepared for starting school.

The child

She is fresh-faced and bouncy, the sort of little girl brought into our homes in the television and newspaper advertisements. Celia is a rather slight, healthy-looking, dark-haired child who skips rather than walks and punctuates her chatter with giggles and grins. The impression the child's physical appearance and demeanour give seem compatible with some comments her mother made when asked to describe her. 'Very independent. Usually happy, except when she's ill. Always on the go – of the three children she's the most active.'

Celia seems to be the sort of child any adult who enjoyed and encouraged children's company would relish. She is chatty, sociable, bright and eager with that engaging sense of fun and inquisitiveness characteristic of many children in this age group. Indeed Celia's mother did maximize the opportunity to enjoy this child as her entry to school, the day after her fifth birthday, marked the first time this pair had been apart, for any length of time, apart from the occasional out-patient visit to hospital by the mother.

Celia had been ill several times, particularly in the winter, with colds and sometimes croup. She had visited hospital because she had had a number of fits, when apparently she 'goes out like a light'. She had not, however, been diagnosed as epileptic and medical opinion was that she would grow out of them. These fits caused her mother considerable concern and she mentioned them as something she would wish to inform the school about.

The pre-school experience

Before Celia went to school she spent much of her time at home with her mother – bouts of housework and relaxation being interrupted by trips to the shops and short excursions, for example to feed a horse kept locally. One summary of activities recorded over one and a half hours.

12.00 – Plenty of activity this morning
a) physical game with mother
b) two TV programmes
c) music from tape/radio
d) discussion about Jack Frost and what frost is. Celia went out to investigate frost on the grass
e) plenty of conversation, both during programmes and activities
f) crayoning
g) puzzle, involving putting pegs in small holes in a pattern
h) laying the table for lunch

This is fairly typical of how Celia spent her time. In a home containing a large collection of board games, colouring books, crayons, toys to stimulate imaginative play and story books, play with such equipment was supplemented by periods of interaction with the mother of a social or work type. Barbara Tizard has suggested (in a talk given to the Association of Child Psychology and Psychiatry, 7.5.80) that she knows of no evidence to support the idea that toys are essential to enhance development or that children and adults should interact through play. As she suggests, there may be other valuable types of interaction, and Celia and her mother seem to illustrate in their home life what forms these interactions could take.

For this child cleaning the oven became a learning experience where the mother seemed to take delight in her efforts to help and to enjoy her company. As Celia vigorously scrubbed the oven door her mother gave encouragement, discussed why the oven was dirty and sympathized when Celia said that all this hard work was making her arm ache. Topics discussed in television programmes were often extended in the home –

'look at these lorries Celia, they're big'. The conversation was extended to include details of lorries seen while out shopping the other day. Celia's mother spoke warmly of her child – 'very thoughtful, unselfish, quite mature for her age, her ideas and how she describes things', and this warmth was reflected in their interactions.

Celia's mother seemed to have well-thought-out opinions about child-care based on intuition and experience. She was sensitive to Celia's needs and used consistent reinforcements of praise and expressions of interest to encourage the child in various activities. The rapport fostered by their relationship minimized the need for discipline and the mother reported that Celia 'hates me to be cross with her'. Rare instances of 'naughtiness' were dealt with by the child being sent to her room until she promised to behave and then being allowed out to be cuddled and loved. The mother's intuitive behavioural programme appeared to facilitate a relationship that both participants found satisfying and rewarding. However they arrived at this treatment, it was a skilful use of a method that has considerable professional support.

It all sounds very straightforward. A child at home full-time with a mother who provides a secure, warm, stimulating environment that both enjoy. Indeed it is difficult to see any pitfalls even when one bears in mind the oft-reported needs of the under-fives and the importance of pre-school provisions. What are the issues raised? Socializing with other children, mixing with adults other than Mum, playing with equipment not normally found in homes, relieving Mum or enabling her to work. None of these seem applicable in this case – indeed the mother's decision not to send Celia to one of the playgroups in the area was taken precisely because, after visiting one, she felt that Celia wouldn't benefit at all from attending. Celia's social needs were, in her mother's mind, catered for by her siblings and by the gang of children aged four to 11 with whom she frequently played. This group of local children, apparently, often ended up in the home and Celia seemed to be totally at ease and friendly – 'she loves birthday parties.' The mother felt that Celia took a little while to relax with new adults, but that she was at ease with the neighbours, at least one of whom visited the home daily.

It seems that despite the fact that she felt under external pressure to do so, Celia's mother had not taken this child to a playgroup for reasons she could identify and substantiate. She seemed to have an intuitive grasp of what could be expected of a child of this age and what sort of expectations the school would have. Colours, the time, shapes, size and number were some of the points slipped regularly into the conversation.

Perhaps what was most striking about this mother was her ability to see the world through a child's eyes – helped no doubt by her obvious delight in the mind of the developing child. On one occasion as Celia went out to the garden to feed the birds her mother remarked with a smile, 'Oh she'll be ages. She tears the bread into really tiny pieces, so that the birds don't choke!'

As perhaps could be expected, the mother had given considerable thought as to how Celia would take to school and had a definite policy of preparation revolving mainly around making positive comments about school and its potential benefits. As mother and child played together – dot-to-dot drawing, a spelling game, colouring – Celia would be told about school, for example, 'when you go to school you'll learn to spell and be able to do this game properly'.

The mother's positive attitude towards the school was reflected in the frequent visits she'd made there as a helper and by her detailed knowledge of the layout and routine of the school. This knowledge, combined with her perception of the child's needs, resulted in 'chats' about the toilet arrangements, the need to put a coat on at playtime, where the library and classroom are and the possibility of bringing home a painting. The possible confusions and unfamiliarities of the school were frequently discussed so that the mother was able to comment that she felt Celia would 'adjust beautifully' and that as 'she knows she's going to be away from me and that school is for children not mummies', there would be no separation problems.

From the mother's point of view the child had been told about school and was prepared. As far as she was concerned she'd stay at school on the first few days and let Celia get involved before slipping away. As she suggested 'they are absorbed and before they know it, it's home time'. Celia, for her part, seemed to be pleased to be going in that she would then be like the others as a member of a 'big' school, and she appeared in her mother's eyes 'raring to go'. On their shopping expeditions they passed the school and Celia would announce proudly that that was 'her' school.

School entry

The much-awaited first day at school:

8.56: Celia and her mother walk into the school porch. Celia looks very small, new and bewildered. She wears a very smart red coat and navy trousers. Hair washed and brushed so that it shines very brightly. Mother talks to another woman, Celia looks around her. Celia holds onto her mother's hand but they don't speak. Mother seems to be enjoying chatter. Celia talks briefly to an older child, but mostly just stands and gazes around her.

9.00: Bell goes. Mother takes Celia's hand and walks through the door with her. Three new children and mothers walk to the classroom. Greeted by the teacher who tells them to sit in the book corner until the other children arrive. Celia sits at the table and starts to do the jigsaw in front of her. Asks mother for help. Seems bemused. Does most of the jigsaw.

9.02: Boy Celia met on her pre-school visit told to take her and her mother to the cloakroom to show Celia where to put her coat. Celia goes off quite happily with this boy. Mother walks behind. Mother takes her coat off, they hang it up.

9.10: Back in classroom, teacher tells mothers to come and pick the children up from the classroom so that they don't get lost. Mother says she will and goes. Celia sits on the floor. Teacher starts a conversation about a boy's birthday and another teacher arrives and says it's assembly, class troops out.

It's now 9.12 a.m. and Celia is in the large hall for assembly. This is her first real taste of school – she's arrived at this much-thought-about place and Mum's gone. As the children stand to sing a hymn the tears come. Celia stands in the crowd holding her arm up across her face and her body starts to shake. The boy she's been paired with tries to comfort her, but to no avail. Her teacher moves towards her and is directed by the head to leave her and 'not to worry', as she's all right.

This initial session in the hall seemed, at the time, to cause Celia considerable distress and there were more long-term effects. As her mother commented . . . 'she was so vulnerable and tiny and she was just left and had to get on with it. About the third day she got up to run out of the hall and a teacher shouted at her and she was terrified. She must have felt awful as she hates drawing attention to herself. She must have felt awful to get up like that'.

Celia's outburst in the hall seemed to set a pattern for the first few days. She didn't want to go back in the afternoon, after lunch, and tears in the morning reached such a pitch that her mother arranged for a neighbour to take her. In the mother's eyes Celia found this a comfort as 'she felt she was leaving me rather than me leaving her, whereas for the teacher Celia was 'holding us to ransom' and 'blackmailing'.

Indeed the attitudes of the two adults involved provide an interesting contrast. The mother felt that she had taught Celia all she could and that she was prepared for school, but that she did not meet with an atmosphere that could capitalize on this. As she suggested, 'I don't feel she had the understanding that she could have had. The other teacher was great and looking back that's probably why there is this trouble. I could stay for two hours before if I wanted to. I had to prise Celia off my arm and leave her.' The teacher commented, 'she was obviously very unsure and unhappy and missed her Mum. I did have nine others (new entrants over three days) so there wasn't much time for her. I just remember she was loath to leave Mum'. This comment was fairly typical of the teacher who tended to see children under stress as misbehaving. In this way by appearing to be child-centred she was merely projecting attention onto the child whereas the focus might more usefully have been on the school.

Behaviour in school

A week later there was evidence to suggest that Celia's extreme distress was situation-specific. Celia had shown no signs of distress this day, in fact her teacher had commented that there was now 'less fuss'. She had done a drawing and been sociable having had lots of chats and giggling with one girl in particular.

> 10.45: End of playtime. Children told to take off their coats and go into the hall. Celia knows where to put her coat. She hangs it up. Wanders alone, does seem rather lost. Has lost the boy whom she played with throughout playtime. As she turns to walk into the hall Celia starts to cry – looks very flushed. She grabs a bigger girl who's walking past and this girl walks into the hall with her – they don't speak.
> When they enter the hall – incredible noise, very loud 'Grand Old Duke of York'. Celia looks scared. They do another song and Celia attempts the actions. Crying stops after about three minutes. It's much quieter now. Class told to go back to room. Celia sits straining, looking for teacher, doesn't cry.

The indications are that Celia's distress was specific to the hall, indeed to the crowded hall, as she coped easily with doing PE there with her class. This point is strengthened by the comment from her mother that Celia was always more distressed in the mornings than after lunch – assembly always being in the mornings.

Although for the first half term in school Celia had had only two full weeks attendance she had adjusted well to the other aspects of school life. She had been ill with severe colds and coughs and the teacher felt that this was genuine and commented that notes had been sent to explain the absences. According to her teacher Celia was 'academically bright' and was 'reading well up with the class in spite of all the time she'd missed'. Certainly Celia managed to cope easily with all the tasks expected, PE dressing and undressing, reading and colouring presented no problems. She named colours when asked and sorted 'sets' with ease. Indeed her mother commented that initially Celia was 'in a no-man's land' and was 'bored, as she'd ask when she was going to read'.

When specific tasks were completed Celia often wandered around in a rather aimless daze and in a classroom that held little visual or material stimulation she sometimes seemed bored and listless. Celia's socializing before school seemed to bear fruit as she was at ease with her peers and would sometimes initiate games. It was not uncommon for Celia to pass from activity to activity, stopping briefly at each, and during these wanderings she would pause to ask the teacher the all-important questions 'when's it home time?', 'What are we going to do now?,' 'What time is it now?'

Her teacher suggested that 'she's always very anxious to know the time and what's happening. She's anxious to get home always'. The teacher's comment that 'there's no great enthusiasm there' seems questionable as Celia responded to learning experiences with gusto, both at home and school and certainly had expressed great enthusiasm for her entry to this 'grown-up' institution.

According to her mother Celia grew more positive towards school as she began to do work and to read. Celia showed her pride in her ability to read her book at home, where with great self-importance she'd insist on reading aloud to all the other family members – 'she was thrilled and so were we'. The lack of cognitive demands made on Celia initially may have been part of a desire to 'ease the children in', however, emotional demands were clearly made and there seemed to be little sympathy directed to these. For example, Celia's mother suggested that she take her teddy bear to school, 'something she loved as a comfort' and the teacher said that she wasn't to bring it as there was a school rule. In a similar vein the head noted, with satisfaction, that Celia had 'got over her tantrums' and suggested that this may 'well be due to a bit of firm handling'.

Conclusions

Celia was described by her teacher as 'a real all-rounder' and 'a capable child'. She appeared sociable both in school and at home and seemed at ease with adults. It could be suggested that Celia's distress was a result of separation anxiety, but this seems difficult to substantiate. Celia had been carefully prepared and had expected school to be a place where Mum could visit, but not stay. The distress seemed to be situation specific and was carried over to the home, suggesting that it was far-reaching.

During the first two weeks of school Celia went into her parents' bedroom at night to ask why she had to go into the hall. Her mother felt that the distress was deep as 'it didn't matter where we were it played heavily on her mind'. During a family visit to a pantomime Celia had got upset asking about the hall and why she had to go to school and asking whether all children had to go to school.

Celia's behaviour changed dramatically at home after she'd started school. She became more temperamental, more aggressive and was tired. She'd refuse food all day and then would eat voraciously in the evening 'as if with the release of school ending'. Concern over this behaviour prompted her mother to visit the teacher as she felt that such distress could spoil Celia's whole outlook. The mother found this chat disappointing as the teacher appeared to feel that she was worrying too much, even though the mother's concern was prompted by an in-depth knowledge of how the child was behaving. The mother commented 'I felt like a naughty little girl telling tales'. The teacher felt that the distress would eventually stop, but it is essential to ask at what cost. An interpretation of the distress as separation anxiety is not supported by the evidence and directs attention from the possibility that a more sympathetic approach – reciprocal inhibition – would have been more effective than simply ignoring the distress which in behavioural terms is a very crude flooding technique.

It is far too simplistic to describe a preference for home, as opposed to school, as separation anxiety. It may well be a rational desire to be in a more stimulating, warm, responsive environment that is free from traumatic experiences that produce distress bordering on phobic reaction. Celia's mother gave considerable thought to why it was that the start had been so difficult and pondered whether she should have Celia to playgroup, though a search for an explanation looking at the child is only one possibility. A more sympathetic approach from the school staff, based on some reputable theory of child development, may have considerably eased the tensions in the situation.

Her mother summed up her view, 'It had been awful when I started school – I've never got over it and when the others started I was really pleased they hadn't had to go through it. But this time it was awful, just like the old days.' Perhaps Celia should have the last word. When the letter had arrived inviting her and her mother to come for a pre-school visit she had leapt in the air and clapped her hands with glee. After half a term she does a similar action, shouting 'oh goody' on being told that it's Friday and that she doesn't have to go to school tomorrow – 'she's beginning to know the days'.

CHAPTER 14

Conclusions

The aim of this report has been to identify and illustrate some of the critical features of continuity in early education and care, and to suggest practical guidelines for smoothing transition from home or pre-school to school. Transition to school is a necessary change in the young child's experience, and continuity may best be examined by looking at what happens when the change occurs.

When a seedling is transplanted from one place to another, the transplantation may be a stimulus or a shock. The careful gardener seeks to minimize shock so that the plant is re-established as quickly as possible. Similarly, for the child moving from one provision to another, a smooth transition requires that the change is sufficient to be stimulating but not so drastic as to cause shock.

Children, like plants, are different and respond to change in different ways. When they are shocked they may exhibit symptoms such as distress, bewilderment or apathy. Other symptoms may be less easily detected or even suppressed for a time. The symptoms discussed here are limited to those which could be observed or reported and which manifested themselves within six weeks of starting school. Some children appear to settle into school easily with no apparent problems, but the majority do experience difficulty to a greater or lesser extent. Symptoms may appear before, on or after transition. The findings suggest ways in which such symptoms may be treated and shock minimized or avoided.

The potential sources of shock are the discontinuities in the child's experience. Whether the child is transferring from a pre-school provision or straight from home, there are likely to be discontinuities associated with the setting, the curriculum and the people.

The setting

The pre-school settings in which children spend time away from home vary tremendously, ranging from private homes, rented halls, prefabs and conversions to modern purpose-built units. Moreover, factors such as the design of the building, shared occupancy, inadequate storage facilities and lack of safe outdoor play space can impose severe limitations on the provision of equipment, activities and displays. Children then transfer to infant schools which range in design from chains of box-like classrooms with corridors to open-plan modules with shared resource areas. The diversity of young children's learning environments thus makes transitions from one to another as idiosyncratic as the children who make them. Nonetheless, the research revealed certain features which, whatever the setting, are critical for the child. These are:

1. the scale or size of the building and its contents;
2. the range or extent of his territory and the proximity or dispersal of facilities such as toilets and play areas, and
3. organizational constraints on movement around his territory and within his base.

Changes are greatest for children transferring from compact settings such as private houses and small nurseries to extended settings such as corridor-plan schools; and from spacious halls with adult-size tables and chairs to congested classrooms. The former are likely to get lost or confused, find it difficult to walk in line and restrain the impulse to run, and worry about getting to the toilet. The latter may find the limitations on space and movement irksome and have difficulty sitting still. Nor can it be assumed that discontinuity is necessarily least for children transferring from a nursery class to a reception class in the same school, since in many cases they have been insulated from the bigger school beyond the nursery. However, transition is likely to be smoother for the child if pre-school and infant settings are comparable in scale, range and freedom of movement.

Given the limitations of buildings and their design, discontinuities can be minimized by the following strategies:

- providing both pre-schoolers and infants with a secure base of appropriate scale i.e. child-size furniture and child-level displays.

- organizing space within the base so that children have room for movement without disrupting the activities of others, as well as corners for privacy and quiet.

- where school facilities are dispersed, situating the reception class as near the toilets as possible.

- familiarizing the child with his new school before entry by walking past it, pausing to watch the children in the playground, and going inside as often as possible.

- introducing the new entrant *gradually* to the extended range of territory beyond the classroom.

The curriculum

Certain features associated with the curriculum were found to be critical to continuity. These include:

1. The perceived aims and functions of staff in the different provisions, their influence on the range of materials and how they were used. Adults in pre-school provisions expressed various aims: minders and day nursery staff emphasized child care and family support, while playgroup leaders and teachers stressed social experience and practice in the basic skills. However, the distinction between care and education was a blurred one, the chief goal in most provisions being to encourage social independence in the child.

2. Financial and spatial constraints. These, coupled with staff aims and their knowledge of the young child's needs, were all reflected in the provision of materials. There was a wider range of activities, both indoor and out, in nursery education provisions than elsewhere. Many playgroups, despite operating on a shoestring in borrowed premises, offered a good range indoors but sometimes suffered from a lack of outdoor playspace and equipment; some private day nurseries and playgroups were more sparsely equipped and shared with minders the constraints of money, space and inadequate storage. Reception classes usually contained at least some of the basic nursery elements such as home corner, sand and floor toys. But a mixed-age class requires a

more extensive range of equipment and unless space is plentiful, materials for the younger child may have to be kept to a minimum.

3. The daily programme. At infant school, the hours away from home are longer for children who have been part-time attenders at pre-school and can cause them fatigue at first. The hours are shorter for children used to all-day care and may pose problems for working mothers. The new entrant is surrounded by a wealth of material, but access to it is restricted by the segmentation of the day into specific activity times and the explicit distinction between work and play. Playtime is usually a compulsory break in the programme when children play in the playground, instead of the more flexible indoor-outdoor play which obtains in most pre-schools. There are also set times for specific activities which may be new to the child, such as PE and assembly.

4. The range of activities. Children in nursery education and playgroups spent more than half their time in three types of activity: spatial, perceptual and fine motor; art and tactile; and imaginative and representational. The groups differed, however, in the fourth major area, gross motor play, since opportunities were more limited in many playgroups. The same activities predominated in day nurseries, but to a lesser extent because more time was taken up with domestic routines. For minded children, equipment-oriented activities occupied a much smaller proportion of the day and there was more emphasis on behaviours which are part of home life like eating, drinking, washing and doing nothing in particular. At infant school, the main pre-school activities no longer predominated. There was a drastic reduction in gross motor activity, which tended to be confined to set periods of PE and playtime; and a considerable increase in activities to do with literacy and numeracy. Discontinuities are likely to be greatest for children who have experienced only a limited range of activities and equipment, and who are unused to handling materials such as books, pencils, scissors, crayons and paint. Problems may also arise for children who have been taught to count extensively by rote, to write numbers and letters in a style different from the school's, and who are already too familiar with the school's early reading scheme.

5. Choice of activity. The greatest discriminator between pre-school and infant activities was the degree of choice children were given in what they did. Children at home or with minders had most freedom of

choice (though from a less extensive range); other pre-schoolers had free choice of available activities for roughly half the time, but this dwindled to less than a quarter at school and was likely to become even less as they got older.

The following strategies may help to minimize curricular discontinuity for the child:

- recognizing the pre-schooler's readiness for more complex tasks and introducing him to some of the activities he will encounter at school.

- giving the child plenty of paper, pencils, crayons, paints and scissors at home, and familiarizing him with books and stories.

- letting him attend school half-days at first, and combating fatigue by allowing him a snack and opportunities to withdraw and look on.

- providing at school some equipment and activities familiar from pre-school, such as play corners, sand and water.

- providing stimulus by gradually expanding the range of new and exciting materials.

- introducing him gradually to new activities, such as PE, and allowing him to watch others from a secure vantage point.

- encouraging parents to support their child's efforts in an *informed* way, particularly in the formation of letters and numbers and the introduction to suitable reading material.

The people

The child starting school is joining a society with larger numbers of children than he has hitherto encountered. The number of children with whom he has to share an adult is likely to be greater than he has ever experienced before. Moreover, the presence at school of large numbers of children and comparatively few adults imposes organizational constraints on both school and class which have important implications for the child, particularly the new entrant. Some of the critical features are:

1. Contact with crowds of children who are older, bigger and noisier than himself, particularly at playtime and dinnertime. Pre-school settings ranged in numbers from one or two children at home with mother or minder to small day nurseries for five or six children, and larger nurseries and playgroups for as many as 30 or 40 children. At infant school, the child could find himself in groups which fluctuated in size from a class of up to 20 or 30 to a crowd of several hundred in assembly, in the playground or at dinner.

2. The presence of few or unfamiliar adults away from the classroom, particularly in the playground, in assembly and at dinner.

3. Organizational procedures which may necessitate lining-up, queueing and waiting. Infants were found to spend three times as much time as pre-schoolers on these 'non-task' activities. This marked increase is mainly a consequence of the need for large numbers of children to move about the building in an orderly manner, of having to take turns with apparatus, and of having to wait for the teacher's attention.

4. Competition for adult attention, which may not only necessitate waiting but also limits opportunities for one-to-one conversation with an adult. Pre-school provisions were found to have a ratio of one adult to not more than 11 children, whereas infant classes had one teacher to as many as 30 children or more. But the presence of adults does not necessarily mean they are involved with the children; they may, for instance, be busy with chores or be supervising passively. Minders and day nursery staff were found to be less often involved with children's activities than adults in playgroups and nursery education. On the other hand, although adults may be busily involved in the children's activities, it is possible for the individual child to receive very little attention personally. In fact, one-to-one situations occupied no more than a very small proportion of time in schools and pre-schools. Contacts were mostly very brief and managerial in content; conversations were more likely to develop with children at home or with a minder.

5. Being addressed as one of a group or class. While children usually make contact with one adult at a time, adults in schools and pre-schools speak not only to individuals but also to groups of all sizes from pairs to the whole unit. For children at home or with minders interactions

were mostly individual, whereas other pre-schoolers were addressed personally only half the time. After transferring to school, there were fewer opportunities for individual interaction with the teacher, and the new entrant had to become accustomed to being addressed with the rest of the class. Although children at pre-school spend much of their time in group situations, the groups tend to be smaller than those encountered at school; some children failed to respond when directions were given to the whole class.

6. Restrictions on movement and noise, and on opportunities for interactive behaviour with other children. Children interacted with each other more at pre-school than at school; after transfer there was a marked increase in parallel behaviour, which accords with the higher incidence of compulsory group and class activities in which the child participates alongside his peers but is passive towards them.

7. Organizational constraints on time, with the possibility of being last or left behind. This was particularly apparent at school dinners and when getting dressed after PE.

Children respond with varying degrees of bewilderment, shyness, distress, impatience or apathy. Discontinuity is likely to be greatest for children coming to school straight from home and for those who have been with a minder or in a very small nursery. These children will have been accustomed to much higher adult–child ratios and, except in extreme cases, will probably have received more personal attention and been less used to being one of a crowd than children in larger provisions. For these children, the presence of masses of strangers can be especially overwhelming. For any new entrant, the presence of an older sibling or friend can be a great source of comfort in new and un-nerving situations. The following strategies may help to minimize the effects of discontinuity:

- keeping the reception class intact and separate at first to allow new entrants to get to know their classmates.
- allowing new entrants to arrive and leave school at a different time from the rest to avoid the crush.
- introducing new entrants gradually to mass events outside the classroom, such as assembly.
- allowing new entrants access to their siblings or friends, or pairing them with an older child, particularly at playtime and dinner.

- providing corners into which new entrants can withdraw, particularly in the playground.
- locating new entrants where they can look on at other children, particularly in assembly.
- having the reception teacher present in new situations like assembly or playtime.
- seating new entrants near the teacher for easy access and attention.
- giving the child pre-school experience in being part of a formal group, with opportunities for listening, responding and behaving appropriately.
- retaining the child's individuality in group situations by using eye contact and calling him by name.
- making use of auxiliary helpers such as parents and older children so that new entrants are not left behind, e.g. getting dressed after PE.

Two events in the infant school day particularly exemplify discontinuity in relation to setting, activity and people, and were found to be powerful sources of potential distress among new entrants. These are playtime and dinnertime.

Playtime represents a major change in the experience of most children starting school. The compulsory timetabled break for play, which is part of the daily pattern in most infant schools, rarely occurs at pre-school where play is not clearly distinguished from other activities. The school playground presents the young child with a territory larger and more crowded than he has encountered at pre-school, and containing little or none of the wheeled and portable equipment to which he has been accustomed. There are signal systems to interpret and sets of procedures for getting there and back. The new entrant is typically a bystander at playtime and his level of activity is low. He is slow to form new friendships and tends to seek out siblings or existing friends. Where these are not available, pairing him with an older pupil can be a successful substitute. Some schools make special arrangements for newcomers in the early days by giving them a separate time or place in which to play, more toys and play equipment, and their own teacher or auxiliary to look after them. The longer dinnertime play period can pose problems of loneliness and boredom, particularly for those who stay to dinner from the start with no siblings or friends present.

Staying to dinner may be a new experience for children who have not been full-time attenders at pre-school, and the food, the cutlery and the system may present problems. Difficulties were found to be clearly related to formality and pressure, and the evidence favours the adoption of a system in which the child has some control over his meal, with minimal constraints on what to eat and how to eat it. The cafeteria system seems best to meet these requirements; the child can select from a range of items and slow eaters can take their time. In many schools new entrants do not stay to dinner till at least their second week.

Personal relationships

So far the discussion has centred on the more obvious sources of discontinuity between pre-school and infant school, and on possible strategies for minimizing their effects. But these are permeated and transcended by personal relationships which, though less easily accessible to the observer's eye or the interviewer's ear, are probably the most important factor in effecting continuity and providing the key to a smooth transition.

The child starting school may be leaving behind warm and secure relationships with adults at pre-school; he may also be leaving his friends. He has to form new relationships with people at school. Throughout this disruption his family remain a constant, and transition is considerably eased for new entrants if siblings or friends are there too.

Relationships at school

The relationships which become crucial when a child starts school are: his relationship with his teacher, his relationship with his peers, and his teacher's relationship with his parents. There are certain features which are particularly critical at the start, when sensitive relationships can be vital. These include:

1. Admission and entry procedures. Local education authorities vary in their policies for admitting children to school and the age of new entrants can range from just four in some areas to almost five and a half in others. It is not clear whether starting age is related to the problems children can encounter; in our sample, difficulties of some kind were experienced across the age range. Children may be admitted every term, twice a year or annually. Actual procedures for entry are largely a matter for the head teacher and vary from school to school. New entrants may be admitted all together, in batches spread over

several days or weeks, or one at a time throughout the same day or week or on their birthday. These procedures have implications for the class which the child is entering: the class may consist entirely of new entrants, or it may build up gradually over a period of days, weeks or months. On the other hand, the class may already be in existence, consisting of pupils who began terms or even years earlier; as new entrants join it the older pupils move on. Thus a child starting school can be one of a small group or a whole class of new entrants, or can be joining a class of older and more experienced pupils.

2. Arrival and induction, with consequent separation from mother and friends and being surrounded by strangers. First impressions are important and the child's welcome can be crucial to his settling in. Where distress occurs, it may appear at the start or later. We found that distress was more likely to occur at the start where large numbers were admitted together, where there was noise and congestion, and where new entrants had to wait some time for personal attention. Children were less likely to be distressed where they were admitted one at a time in a calm unhurried atmosphere, where mother and child were welcomed personally, where there was time for a chat with the teacher and the mother could linger if she wished. The child's personal sense of importance was encouraged by the allocation of his own coatpeg and drawer with his name and a picture on for easy recognition; in some cases he was also given a name badge to wear so that others could more easily identify him. Toys and activities were usually set out ready, and the child was either allotted a task by the teacher, or allowed to explore or look on at others.

3. Pre-entry visits and the exchange of information. Most infant heads arrange for children and their parents to visit the school at least once before entry and, less commonly, a series of visits is encouraged. Some children have also called at the school incidentally with their older siblings. More rarely, the staff of neighbouring playgroups and nurseries are invited to bring the new entrants to see the school or attend special events. Children transferring from a nursery unit or class in the same school are more likely to have some familiarity with the infant building and staff, though in some cases the class or unit is so self-contained as to have almost no association with the rest of the school. Visits are usually made the term before entry, thus creating a time lapse during the school holidays of up to two months for September

starters. Only two-thirds of the teachers in the sample recalled having seen the child before entry. Very few teachers were familiar with their pupils' pre-schools, though in some cases the infant head had visited local groups. Reception teachers tended to have only minimal information about their new pupils; when it was available many teachers chose to ignore it, preferring to form their own opinions about each child. Others would have liked to be better informed about medical problems or specific difficulties which could affect the child's school behaviour. Information passed on from pre-schools ranged from written reports to verbal exchanges and tended to be haphazard in availability and content. More structured information was received from nursery education staff, often in the form of county record cards which covered abilities and skills, language development and temperament. Parents were asked to supply their child's basic biographical details on an admission form.

4. Getting to know each other. The developing of relationships between teacher and pupil and between pupil and peers is a complicated process the mechanisms of which are not always observable. Much depends on the teacher's skill in establishing rapport, on the personalities of teacher and child, and on the teacher's relationship with the other children in the class. However, the study revealed that new entrants have specific needs which are particularly important on the first day and which can be met with warmth and sensitivity. These include: a) a friendly environment, created not only by an attractive physical setting, but, more importantly, by an atmosphere of calm within the classroom and the avoidance of sudden loud noises and raised voices; the teacher's tone of voice is important and some newcomers get upset when the teacher reprimands other pupils; b) frequent short bursts of individual attention and reassurance, both when carrying out prescribed tasks and when participating in more formal group situations; and c) the need for support in front of strangers: the newcomer is particularly susceptible to the risk of 'losing face' by behaving inappropriately, and to embarrassment sustained in coping with unfamiliar toilets or undressing for PE; support from both adults and peers is important to his self-esteem.

5. The bombardment of new sights and sounds, unfamiliar words and strange procedures. The new entrant encounters much that can baffle and even frighten him at first and which is taken for granted by staff

and older pupils: bells, buzzers or hooters, and noisy urinals; words, phrases and directives like 'home base' and 'make a line'; the role of adults other than his teacher, such as dinner lady and welfare assistant; patterns of behaviour for going out to play or getting ready for lunch. He needs explanations which are sensitive but not overwhelming.

6. Introduction to work tasks. Sooner or later the pupil is introduced to 'work', a specific task usually related to literacy or numeracy. Ability varied considerably among new entrants and appeared to relate not only to pre-school experience but also to the opportunity of having practised at home. Work brings with it the notion of 'getting it right' and the child learns success and failure. Initial efforts require sensitive treatment and rewards usually take the form of praise and progression to new books. On completing a task, new entrants exhibited varying degrees of uncertainty about what to do next, especially if given free choice.

7. Introduction to new activities. Routines and patterns of appropriate behaviour, such as how to move from place to place in an orderly manner, and when to keep still and silent, have to be learned for specific events like assembly, PE, and music and movement, which take place away from the classroom. At assembly the people and surroundings are less familiar, proceedings may follow a particular sequence, words and tunes have to be memorized; PE and movement require the removal of certain items of clothing without embarrassment and the ability to cope with fastenings, as well as the introduction of new apparatus and procedures for using it.

8. Patterns of attendance. For most children, starting school brings a change in the length of time they are away from home. Many of those who have been in all-day care are accustomed to longer hours, and the shorter school day creates problems for working mothers who may have to make arrangements for their child to be cared for after school. But for the majority who have attended playgroups and nursery classes for half-days only, the school day is longer; nursery rest-time is seldom continued at school and fatigue is commonly reported. Hours of attendance for new entrants were found to vary from full-time from the start to mornings only for the first week or so. Some infant schools operate a shorter day by dispensing with afternoon playtime or shortening the dinner break. Some children who coped happily with their

first day at school were less enthusiastic when they realized they had to go every day, and expressed reluctance or hankered after their pre-school. Parents and teachers quickly overcame this with firm and sensitive handling. However, distress was triggered in some apparently settled children by a period of absence, an accident or a home upset in the early weeks.

The development of sensitive relationships will help to mitigate or even avoid distress, and the following strategies are likely to create a favourable climate in which these can develop from the start:

- arranging for the child and his parents to visit the school frequently before entry to meet staff and children.

- staggering entry, with a personal welcome for each child and his escort.

- being prepared for the new entrant: having his peg and drawer ready; knowing his name, his pre-school experience and his problems.

- strengthening teacher–child bonds by using eye-contact, calling the child by name and having plenty of time for him.

- giving him a calm start, and reducing noise and loud commands to a minimum.

- reassuring him with plenty of praise and frequent short bursts of attention.

- supporting him in front of others and sparing him embarrassment.

- explaining unfamiliar sights, sounds and events; showing him around; and introducing him to other adults he will meet.

- being extra sensitive to him after critical incidents such as accidents, home upsets, and absence of teacher or child.

- giving the new entrant opportunities to make new friends in class and encouraging the older children to be caring and supportive.

- encouraging cooperation between parents and teacher, and providing early opportunities to exchange information which might affect the child and to discuss his progress.

The family and the school

The three main agents in the child's transition are the pre-school, the infant school and the home, and the child who has supportive relationships in all three is most likely to make a smooth transition. His family can be a powerful mediator of continuity, particularly if there are older siblings already at school. But most contacts between parents and staff in both schools and pre-schools were fleeting, occurring on arrival and departure. Few of the sample parents had been actively involved in their child's pre-school, apart from fund-raising or helping at special events. They regarded transition as a step from play to 'proper learning' and they viewed it with some trepidation which they tried to conceal from their children. Mothers described it as a milestone in their lives and feelings ranged from sadness to relief; family routines were adjusted to cope with changes in the child's eating and sleeping patterns. Most parents expressed a desire to know more about what goes on in schools, but seemed to sense barriers of professionalism and kept their distance, despite invitations by several schools to visit at any time. By the end of the first month, parents would have welcomed an opportunity to discuss their child's progress, but teachers did not express the same urgency and parents were reluctant to appear interfering. All the parents had received paper communications of some kind from the school and many had been offered opportunities for fund-raising or participating on the fringes. But these are neither necessary nor sufficient conditions for the development of parent-teacher relationships. Personal contact of a more than fleeting nature is essential, and creating opportunities for this after the child starts school may be too late since mothers are already planning their futures and returning to work. If positive relationships are to be established between home and school, they must be begun before the child starts. To this end, at least one school encouraged a steady build-up of pre-entry visits for parent and child over a period of several weeks. The success of such a strategy, however, depends on a willing staff and cooperative interested parents.

Parents suggested that schools could make life easier for new entrants by:

- allowing the children to visit more often before the start.

- showing them around and explaining where everything is.

- encouraging them to ask when they do not know something.

- letting parents accompany their child into the classroom on arrival and allowing him to wait indoors till collected.

- having someone look after the new ones at playtime, and being lenient on their eating habits at dinner.

Staff in schools and pre-schools suggested that parents could prepare their child for school by:

- encouraging a positive attitude, whetting his appetite and regarding school as a privilege, not a threat.

- teaching him to dress himself, cope with the toilet, and speak up for himself.

- accustoming him to being away from his mother.

- talking and reading to him to extend his vocabulary.

- taking an interest in what he does without putting pressure on him.

Outcomes

When a child starts school there are certain features about the building, the curriculum, the people and personal relationships which are critical to the continuity of his experience. There was no evidence from this study to suggest that starting age is crucial; difficulties were experienced across the age-range. Children who had attended two pre-schools concurrently before transfer settled into school without any notable problems. Children who appeared to settle most easily had older siblings who had attended the same school and opportunities at home for using pencils, crayons and books. Minor misunderstandings between parents and teachers did not always appear to have any immediate or deleterious effect on the child. Children from each type of pre-school provision experienced a variety of difficulties or none at all. A period of absence could trigger symptoms of distress in a hitherto settled child.

The immense variety of pre-school experience, together with the temperamental predisposition of children to react differently, makes each child's transition unique. Yet the research demonstrates that three ingredients are essential if shock is to be reduced to a minimum:

1. Changes and the introduction of new experiences must be *gradual* rather than sudden.
2. People, places and things must be to some extent *familiar* rather than totally strange.
3. The child must have a sense of *security* rather than instability.

Many people are aware that starting school is a momentous event in a child's life and the research has revealed some of the strategies employed to make it pleasurable. But the study has also revealed considerable gaps in understanding:

Parents who do not appreciate the place of pre-schools in the learning process, who do not know what goes on in schools today, and who want to help their child but are not sure how.

Pre-school staff who do not know what goes on in other provisions, who would like more contact with schools and who feel their opinions are not valued.

Infant staff who know nothing of their new entrants' pre-school experience, who regard pre-schools with suspicion, who seem unapproachable to parents and non-professionals, and who are unaware of the cultural customs of their pupils.

The child's experience is a link between pre-school, infant school and family; yet while he interacts with each of them, they may have little or no contact with each other. They all work in the child's interest, yet may know little or nothing of each other's work.

There are many individuals who do strive for wider understanding: teachers who visit playgroups, heads whose schools are always open to parents and visitors, day nurseries which involve the whole family. But these efforts, while commendable, are parochial and individualistic; and there are always practical problems. What is required is a more concerted attempt on a wider scale to bring together everyone involved in early education and care, so that they can learn more about each other's aims and work.

In 1976 and 1978, official joint letters were issued by the DES and DHSS encouraging local authorities to set up procedures to coordinate the various pre-school services. Prior to this, nursery centres had already been opened in some authorities where day care and education could proceed side by side and which were jointly administered by the social services and education departments. Other attempts at coordination were encountered during this study: teachers visiting playgroups for half a day per week; teachers employed to work part-time in a group of day nurseries;* courses run by LEAs, the social services and the Pre-school Playgroups Association for anyone interested in the under-fives. But attempts at coordination so far tend to be spasmodic and piecemeal, varying from one local authority to another, and those operating in our sample areas were not sufficiently developed for their effect on target children to be assessed.

The Schools Council project 'Transition and Continuity in Early Education' in 1978 set up and monitored a series of experimental liaison groups. Each group consisted of people who were involved in the care and education of young children in a neighbourhood: teachers, nursery nurses, childminders, playgroup staff, parents and health visitor. The groups met regularly to share their experiences, discuss their work and explore ways of smoothing transition between provisions. The groups proved to be useful in bringing together adults with widely different attitudes. The parents were willing, on the whole, to do anything which would help the children, especially their own; day nursery staff were delighted to be included, and exchange views and ideas with others; playgroup staff were generally open-minded and expressed a willingness to learn; childminders were cautious; teachers regarded the meetings as a course which would enrich their work. The professionalism of teachers, however, tends to be seen as a barrier by parents and non-professionals; teachers are regarded as experts and they are aware that their comments may be taken as advice. Professional training and in-service courses could, perhaps, play an important role in familiarizing teachers, and nursery nurses too, with the work of others in their field.

Clearly, there is a need for everyone concerned with young children to learn about each other's work and visit each other's provision. Barriers of suspicion, professional jealousy and entrenched attitudes must be broken

---

*The Education Act of 1980 states that LEAs may make available to local authority day nurseries the services of teachers employed by them in nursery schools or primary schools with nursery classes.

down in the interests of cooperating together for the benefit of the child. This applies not only at a general level, but also at the personal level of the child and the relationships between his parents, his pre-school and his school. If real understanding is to be achieved at either level, three things are required: an open mind; a willingness to learn, and the ability to appreciate another's point of view.

Appendix

Appendix: Chapter 5

Table A: Activities: Percentage of time spent in each activity by 36 children in their last six weeks at pre-school and first six weeks at infant school.

Activity no. of children	Infant classes 36	Nursery units 12	Nursery school 3	Play-groups 15*	Day nurser-ies 6	Child-minder 1	Home 1
Gross motor	7.3	7.0	20.5	12.3	15.9	.8	1.7
Spatial, perceptual and fine motor	6.8	6.6	8.8	12.2	11.0	10.0	2.5
Art and tactile	8.1	11.1	6.3	8.5	12.9	25.8	24.2
Musical	4.4	8.8	4.0	4.3	4.6	3.1	.8
Imaginative and representational	4.7	10.2	5.4	9.2	4.8	23.5	3.3
Verbal and symbolic	24.7	21.1	19.8	13.0	6.3	6.2	28.5
Understanding the physical world	.3	1.2	2.5	1.0	1.4	11.5	3.3
Activity prep. and termination	4.1	4.8	6.0	4.9	2.4	2.3	8.3
Domestic routine	9.5	9.0	3.5	6.4	7.5	3.8	8.3
Waiting	12.3	9.7	4.2	12.4	9.9	6.9	.8
Watching	3.7	3.0	4.2	4.4	7.6	—	5.0
Cruising	9.1	4.4	5.6	5.4	7.3	2.3	4.2
Social expression (neutral/positive)	4.8	3.0	9.0	5.4	8.2	3.8	8.3
Social expression (negative)	.2	.1	.2	.6	.2	—	.8

* one child attended playgroup and nursery unit
   one child attended playgroup and childminder

Appendix: Chapter 5:

Table B: Choice: Percentage of time spent in each mode of choice by 36 children in their last six weeks at pre-school and first six weeks at infant school.

Provision	No Choice	Limited Choice	Free Choice	No. of Children
Infant class	67.7	8.5	23.8	36
Nursery units	57.7	1.0	41.3	12
Nursery school	29.2	8.5	62.3	3
Playgroups	40.3	2.5	57.2	15*
Day nurseries	34.2	13.9	51.9	6
Childminder	6.9	0.8	92.3	1
Home	9.2	4.2	86.6	1

* one child attended playgroup and nursery unit
  one child attended playgroup and childminder

Appendix: Chapter 6

Table C: Number of children present: Percentage of time for which specific numbers of children were present with target children in the different provisions.

No. of children	1–5	6–10	11–15	16–20	20+
Provision					
Infant class	1.8	2.4	7.5	33.3	55.0
Nursery unit	0.7	2.7	5.4	13.6	77.6
Nursery school		12.2			87.8
Playgroup				11.7	88.3
Day nursery	0.7	2.8	37.2	24.8	34.5
Childminder	100.0				
Private home	100.0				

References

BRUNER, J. (1980). *Under Five in Britain*. Oxford Preschool Research Project. Grant McIntyre.

CENTRAL ADVISORY COUNCIL FOR EDUCATION (ENGLAND), (1967). Children and their Primary Schools (Plowden Report) London: HMSO.

CLIFT, P., CLEAVE, S., and GRIFFIN, M. (1980). *The Aims, Role and Deployment of Staff in the Nursery*. Windsor: NFER.

GREAT BRITAIN. DEPARTMENT OF EDUCATION AND SCIENCE (1972). *Education: A Framework for Expansion*. London: HMSO. Circular 2/73 to local education authorities.

GREAT BRITAIN. (1975c). *Nursery Education* (DES Report on Education No. 81). London: DES.

GREAT BRITAIN. (1975) *Pre-School Education and Care. Some Topics Requiring Research or Development Projects*. London: DES.

GREAT BRITAIN. DEPARTMENT OF EDUCATION AND SCIENCE, joint letter with Department of Health and Social Security (March 1976). Co-ordination of Local Authority Services for Children under Five. Ref. No: DES S214765.

GREAT BRITAIN. DEPARTMENT OF EDUCATION AND SCIENCE, joint letter with Department of Health and Social Security (January 1978). Co-ordination of Services for Children under Five. Ref: No: DES S47/24/013.

GREAT BRITAIN. DEPARTMENT OF EMPLOYMENT (1977). 'New projections of labour force.' *DES Gazette*, **6**, 587.

GREAT BRITAIN. MINISTRY OF EDUCATION. *Circular 8/60*.

GREAT BRITAIN. MINISTRY OF HEALTH. *Circular 37/68*.

HUGHES, MAYALL, MOSS, PERRY, PETRIE and PINKERTON (1980). *Nurseries Now. A fair deal for parents and children*. Harmondsworth: Penguin Books.

JOSEPH, A. and PARFIT, J. (1972). *Playgroups in an area of social need*. A National Children's Bureau Booklet. Windsor: NFER.

KELLMER PRINGLE, M. (1974). *The Needs of Children*. Hutchinson & Co.

MORGAN, G. A. V., HOFSTRA, G., BLACK, E. and SKINNER, L. (1979). *Children's Characteristics on School Entry*. Ontario: Ministry of Education.

PARRY, M. and ARCHER, H. (1974). *Pre-school Education*. Macmillan Education.

PRE-SCHOOL PLAYGROUPS ASSOCIATION (1980). *Report on Parental Involvement in Playgroups*. PPA.

SMITH, T. (1980). *Parents and Preschool*. Oxford Preschool Research Project. Grant McIntyre.

TAYLOR, P. H., EXON, G. and HOLLEY, B. (1972). Schools Council Working Paper 41. A Study of Nursery Education. Evans/Methuen Educational.

TIZARD, B. (1975). *Early Childhood Education*. A review and discussion of research in Britain. Windsor: NFER.

TIZARD, B., MORTIMORE, J. and BURCHELL, B. (1981). *Involving Parents in Nursery and Infant Schools*. Grant McIntyre.

TOUGH, J. (1976). *Listening to Children Talking: a Guide to the Appraisal of Children's Use of Language*. Schools Council Communication Skills in Early Childhood Project. London: Ward Lock Educational.

WOOD, D., McMAHON, L. and CRANSTOUN, Y. (1980). *Working with Under Fives*. Oxford Preschool Research Project. Grant McIntyre.

WOODHEAD, M. (1976). *Intervening in Disadvantage: A challenge for Nursery Education*. Windsor: NFER.

WOODHEAD, M. (1979). *Pre-school Education in Western Europe: Issues, Policies and Trends*. London: Longman Group Ltd.